Stephens~

Seek Him First!,

Mt 6.33

B Cal

FROM FAITH TO FAITH

Fathers, are you absent or abiding?

Bill C. Dotson

CROSSBOOKS
PUBLISHING

CrossBooks™
A Division of LifeWay
1663 Liberty Drive
Bloomington, IN 47403
www.crossbooks.com
Phone: 1-866-879-0502

First published by CrossBooks: 05/03/2011
ISBN: 978-1-6150-7114-2 (sc)
Library of Congress Control Number: 2010920715

Scripture quotations marked KJV are taken from the Holy Bible, King James Version,
Cambridge, 1769.

Scripture quotations marked NASB from the NEW AMERICAN STANDARD BIBLE®,
©Copyright The Lockman Foundation 1960, 1962, 1963, 1968, 1971, 1972, 1973, 1975,
1977, 1995. Used by permission. All rights reserved. (www.lockman.org)

Scripture quotations marked NKJV from the New King James Version®. Copyright © 1982 by
Thomas Nelson, Inc. Used by permission.

Scripture quotations marked (NIV®) are taken from the HOLY BIBLE, NEW
INTERNATIONAL VERSION®. NIV®. Copyright ©1973, 1978, 1984 by Biblica, Inc.™. Used
by permission. All rights reserved worldwide.

Scripture quotations marked MSG from THE MESSAGE. Copyright © by Eugene H. Peterson
1993, 1994, 1995, 1996, 2000, 2001, 2002. Used by permission of NavPress Publishing Group.

To the Agreement dated August 10, 2010 between ALFRED MUSIC PUBLISHING CO. INC.
and BILL C. DOTSON:
CAT'S IN THE CRADLE
Words and Music by HARRY CHAPIN and SANDY CHAPIN ©1974 (Renewed) STORY
SONGS, LTD. All Rights Administered by WB MUSIC CORP. All Rights Reserved. Used by
Permission of ALFRED MUSIC PUBLISHING CO., INC.

Printed in the United States of America
This book is printed on acid-free paper.

Any people depicted in stock imagery provided by Thinkstock are models,
and such images are being used for illustrative purposes only.

Certain stock imagery © Thinkstock.

CONTENTS

DEDICATION

This book is dedicated to my deceased father, Chester A. Dotson. The longer I have lived, the more I know you loved me and were always proud of me. I have been pleased to be your son. To my mother, Clara, for loving me no matter what. To Joanne, my wife, for making me a better father; to my two children, Becky and Evelyn, for accepting me as their father; to Brad and Sandro for loving our daughters; and to the five grandchildren, Luke, Sarah Peyton, Annie, Will, and Renzo, who make my life as a grandfather so joyous and complete. "Happy is the man who has his quiver full of them" (Ps. 127:5).

ACKNOWLEDGMENTS

I want to thank all those who contributed to this book. Thanks to Dudley Hall for his foreword and to the men in my life who shared their testimonies about fatherhood. In no particular order, they are Ronald Sellers, Arthur Wood, Arrvel Wilson, Ford Madison, Len McLaughlin, and Kurt Nelson. Thanks to my daughter Evelyn, who was a helpful editor. Thanks to Joanne, who encouraged me and laid the groundwork to get me started writing. Thanks to CrossBooks Publishing for helping me through the process. Thanks to the Lord who encouraged me to write it through the prompting of His Holy Spirit. And thanks to all you men who will read it and take the steps to become an *"abiding father."*

FOREWORD

When a man of passion takes a pen in his hand to unload his heart, the wise take heed. It is not easy to write in such a way that busy people will read, so I appreciate the commitment Bill Dotson has made to address one of the most vital subjects in our society.

When statistics are quoted that reveal the fatherlessness in our world, the most common response is denial. We just can't believe it is so rampant. Surely the pollsters aren't counting correctly. Then we tend to wonder if it really matters. It is so epidemic; we are paralyzed by its force and try to convince ourselves that the original design of the home is not essential. In a politically correct environment, we shy away from even suggesting that somebody might be doing something dangerously wrong. We continue to allow conflicted men to ignore their calling, while frustrated women struggle with the dynamic of their absent partners. Though not living in planned orphanages, millions of children grow up with orphaned hearts and by default, view life through orphaned eyes. Fearful of never being enough, they are vulnerable to high levels of anxiety and relational conflict. Never sure they have done enough to gain the status of sons, they are targets of perfectionism—or the opposite, passivity. This fatherless mentality will make it difficult for them to relate in a healthy way to God or His creation.

Bill is aware that just restoring the home is not the goal. Even if we could restore it to Eden-like status, men and women would still suffer from being alienated from the original Father. The only lasting solution is for individuals to find reconciliation to God the Father through the mediation of His Son. As we discover the security of being loved unconditionally by none other than God the Father, we are free to venture into risky endeavors of cultural transformation. The gospel is the only hope of permanent change. We are all orphans until the Son introduces us to the Father. There is no room for finger pointing. Even the best of homes cannot adequately display the exquisite nature of Father and Son. Only Jesus has done that, and He is ready to give that relationship to any who will trust Him.

As you read Bill's words, you will hear the heart of a man in the marketplace who has made the connection with the kingdom of God. Though not an ecclesial minister, he is busy making sure he has managed the garden God has given to him. He speaks as one who is in the midst of life. These are no mere observations of a spectator. He cares about what he is saying, because he cares for those to whom he speaks.

May you be informed and stirred by what you read.

Dudley Hall
President of Successful Christian Living Ministries
Author: *Grace Works, Incense and Thunder, Glad to be Left Behind, Men in Their Own Skin*

PREFACE TO
FROM FAITH TO FAITH

"It is not the critic who counts; not the man who points out how the strong man stumbles, or where the doer of deeds could have done them better. The credit belongs to the man who is actually in the arena, whose face is marred by dust and sweat and blood; who strives valiantly; who errs, who comes short again and again, because there is no effort without error and shortcoming; but does actually strive to do the deeds; who knows great enthusiasms, the great devotions; who spends himself in a worthy cause; who at the best knows in the end the triumph of high achievement, and who at the worst, if he fails, at least fails while daring greatly, so that his place shall never be with those cold and timid souls who neither know victory nor defeat."[1]

—Theodore Roosevelt

Twenty-plus years ago, the Lord placed on my heart a burden that is near and dear to His heart, which, ashamedly I have not dealt with until now. *Fathers* are men who have been blessed with the joy of children, along with the earthly responsibility of raising, nurturing, and equipping them to become responsible and productive beings. While I wrote a plan for challenging fathers as I believed I had been shown, it is not until now that I have acted on the call. Recently, I was led to pull out the old notes, dust them off, refresh the thoughts, and share them with my family and friends.

As I write this preface, I truly do not know where this is going, but I do know I *must* write what is on my heart and mind. I am privileged to be a father of two wonderful young ladies, now mothers of our five marvelous grandchildren. While my birth name is Billy Cleveland, I am now affectionately called Bumpa. My wife, Joanne, is now Gami. To us, this is who we are. And quite frankly, we love it.

As I was starting to prepare for this writing journey, Joanne purchased several "how to" books on publishing. One stated that there is at least one good book in everyone. Well, the following chapters are mine. I must write about what I believe to be, by far, the most significant tragedy in America, and it has become, increasingly, a severe situation. It is the basic root problem in the majority of our lives today: *the absence of fathers in the home.*

What I have witnessed and experienced as a son, grandson, father, and now, grandfather has shaped my view of the world of the family. Simply, a relational God, Creator, has established a means for people to grow and prosper as He intended. This means is a family—a father, mother, and children, and from there, the extended family. The health of a family falls primarily on the parents, but most of the responsibility has been laid at the feet of the husband/father. When embraced, the family has the greatest chance of succeeding in its intended purpose.

While I am an evangelical Christian, who has placed my trust in Jesus Christ for my salvation, I must say up front that what the following pages address is true for Christians or non-Christians. The facts are the same for all, as well as the responsibilities and ultimate results. This book is intended for fathers or would-be fathers. My warning to both is that the role is not to be taken lightly but seriously and thoughtfully. Many children are born into this world to parents, especially fathers, who have not weighed the supreme responsibilities of parenthood. Unless there is a reversal in that, the family is most assuredly destined for failure. Statistics are frighteningly proving this to be the case.

Death and tragedies occur, altering many nuclear homes. These cannot be avoided. But the facts in America today indicate children are being abandoned by fathers at an alarming rate, even while occupying the home. My confession to you, the reader, is that I have made virtually every parental and spousal mistake that has ever been thought of or committed. Confession should always be followed by repentance, with the hope of a fresh start. This book is not an epistle on perfect fatherhood but an analysis of the facts and the means to restore the father in the home, leading as he has been ordained to do.

In my study of the Bible, I really see nothing addressed to the mother about the responsibilities of her role. I find this interesting. But I have concluded that God knew that a woman, whom He created, will instinctively have an affection and deep abiding love for her child. But the man—that appears to be a different story altogether. For instance, I play golf. In the spring, I observe the mating of the duck world. The drake hangs around till the ducklings are born, and then, whammo, he's off. There's the mother duck leading her flock into adulthood without his services. We men are increasingly doing the same.

Having visited and taught in several prison and juvenile centers for years, I have become sadly aware of the lack of any positive influence on the residents by their fathers, with many never even knowing them. Death rows are full of men and women who had no, or a horrible, relationship with their father. Drugs, violence, school truancy, homosexuality, suicide, and much more are a result of the father's absenteeism. We all know that gangs are an attempt at a family. The majority of these kids are acting out of the fact they do not have that male role model in their life.

I have the privilege of teaching the Scriptures to men at the Union Gospel Mission in Dallas. Many have shared that their relationship with their father was strained at best. One evening recently, the subject matter turned to the role of fathers and I shared that I was writing a book on the impact of the absence of fathers in the home and the destructive force this is to the family. I have received some nice applause from them at times, but this was a spontaneous and almost thunderous reaction. They knew full well, firsthand, and were in complete agreement. It was an emotional moment for me and I am sure for many of them. *See, every person has a father, but only a few know a father.*

During this time, one man held up his hand. I walked over to hear his question. But what he said to me and the group was this: "I am out on parole, and my children live in Ohio. I plan to go there and see my kids and reconcile my relationship with them." He was moved emotionally. Why? He knew he needed to! I encouraged him, as this is what most of us need to be doing. I hope he does and they forgive each other and start living and prospering as a family. This father is taking the first necessary step: *reconciliation!*

A recent report showed that 40 percent of babies born in America in 2008 were to a single-parent home, and that number climbs to 70 percent in the African-American community.[2] Welfare, convenience, and many other outside negative influences have produced this. This has to change. The pendulum must start swinging in the other direction or else the America that we have known is doomed for collapse from within. It is well underway. A wake-up call needs to be sounded. Alarms are going off all over our nation. Kids are telling us fathers, "You have failed us, you have abandoned us, and you don't even care about us."

None of the above reflects the *millions of* babies who have been aborted before birth in America, most for convenience to promiscuous adults. Life is precious whenever it is conceived.

God made life something to be cherished. It reflects Him and His love. We are created in His image. We have marred the image. But there is hope. Maybe the thoughts in this book will impact you and you will see yourself as a father in an entirely different role. Men, maybe, just maybe, by the grace of God, we can, one by one, reassume our role in the family. It may start with repentance, seeking forgiveness, redirecting priorities, or assuming responsibility. Whatever it requires will be worth all the effort.

Recently, I was privileged to attend a Dallas Prayer Breakfast and hear Brad McCoy, father of Colt McCoy, former quarterback for the Texas Longhorns. Among many enlightening things he expressed that morning was the central thought, which everyone there came away talking about. With his permission, I have reprinted it here, as I think it may just be one of the most profound and thought provoking expressions I have ever heard relative to parenting. He said, *"Do not prepare the path for the child; prepare the child for the path."* He went on to say that he and his wife raised their sons under that umbrella of thought. Brad shared several tenets of their parenting they used that stemmed from and accented this overriding theme. Hopefully, much of what is set out in the following chapters will assist you in making a prophet out of Brad McCoy. From where I stand, it appears their philosophy has worked well.

The title of this book sorta says it all: *From Faith to Faith.* From fathers *absent* in the home to fathers *abiding* in the home. For some this will be a hard journey, while others just need to reawaken right where they are living and assume their role. Men, will you join me now and share the thoughts in the following pages? It won't be all-inclusive, and I bet we have to write a follow-up to this one because we missed so many points that we fathers need to hear and embrace but mainly, because the tide of fatherhood is taking hold in American families and the stories of re-engagement have become overwhelming.

Know that I am praying for that to happen. Heed the words of Mr. Roosevelt and *"Spend yourself in a worthy cause."*[3] **Join me, fathers!**

STATE OF THE FAMILY

As I am writing this, we are facing a crisis of major proportions in the American family. Welfare and poverty in certain segments have all but destroyed the nuclear household. Political and economic pressures have made it convenient to bring children into the world, the ones not aborted before birth, without an inkling of hope that these children will grow up in a well-balanced and managed home setting. While the ethnicity varies somewhat, every class is falling prey: white, Black, Hispanic, Christian, and non-Christian.

During the time that John Emirsch was associated with ESRC Society Today, he featured a study called, "Births Outside Marriage: The Real Story." He is quoted as saying that "Four in ten births are outside marriage, compared with under ten percent a quarter of a century ago. Most of these births, however, are to cohabiting couples, not single mothers."[4] But John Emirsch explains, "The rise in the proportion of births outside marriage should still be a source of serious concern."[5] And he goes on to say, *"There is growing evidence that experience of life in a single-parent family during childhood is usually associated with disadvantageous outcomes as young adults."*[6]

William Julius Wilson, author of *When Work Disappears*, is quoted as saying "that growing rates of single parenthood cut across racial lines, but are most evident in the inner city. The result for children is more poverty, less supervision, and a riskier future."[7]

Added to the above, the divorce rate is climbing each year in every level of society. Most children in these families end up suffering, some more than others, but all in some way are affected. Divorce or separation adds to the mounting number of single mothers. I recently read with interest an article in the *Dallas Morning News* by Lorrie Irby Jackson, a Dallas freelance journalist. The title was, "Moms, Stop Shutting out Dads." With her permission, I have quoted from the article. She states, and I believe accurately, "There is a difference between accepting a hardship and creating one, and that's what some women do when they consciously ban the biological father of their children from participating in those young people's lives." She goes on later to say, "Women cannot be both mothers and fathers to their kids. They may want to, or even attempt to, but they cannot."

Ms. Jackson is right when she states:

> "Without fathers, our sons may look like men, but they follow the warped examples offered by entertainers, athletes or other (in)famous thugs who teach their fans that tearing down women makes someone more of a man. Our daughters end up hungering for male attention and give their hearts—and bodies—to the first man with sweet talk and a smile. Later on, many grow up disillusioned about love and pass this dysfunction on to their own children if no one steps in to break the cycle."

And finally, "Consider this unpleasant reality: Our streets and jails are filled to capacity with fatherless men, while too many strip clubs and abuse shelters are bursting with fatherless women."[8]

Several years ago, our church, along with several others, became involved heavily with the families and their children in West Dallas. In particular, a ministry was birthed: Mercy Street Dallas (www.mercystreetdallas.org). Founder and Executive

Director Trey Hill saw a need, and God gave him a burden for the twenty-four hundred-plus youth in that community. He, his wife, and their four young children moved to the neighborhood, and many of his staff have done the same. Among other valuable programs, Christian mentors for the children from the fourth to twelfth grades are being provided, with the goal and hope of breaking the cycle of dependency and despair in the next few generations. Why are ministries like Mercy Street needed? Primarily because the vital element of the family is missing—*fathers*. Someone is needed to step into the gap for these needy children.

A friend shared the following, which speaks to the results of fatherless families. According to the U. S. Department of Justice, the following reflects how youth are manifesting their hurt and anger in all kinds of destructive ways. Sadly for them and our society, these are our next generation of parents. Most are without any parenting skills. Worse yet, they are severely crippled even before taking on an adult responsibility of raising a family.

63 percent of youth suicides are from fatherless homes

90 percent of all homeless and runaway youths are from fatherless homes

85 percent of children who exhibit behavioral disorders are from fatherless homes

71 percent of high school dropouts are from fatherless homes

71 percent of youths in state institutions are from fatherless homes

75 percent of adolescent patients in substance abuse centers are from fatherless homes

85 percent of rapists motivated by displaced anger are from fatherless homes[9]

In the midst of all these sad statistics and before we lose any semblance of hope, let us focus briefly on the one who gives hope. He is our Savior. "He executes justice for the orphan …" (Deut. 10:18 NASB). Some would translate this to say, "He defends the cause of the fatherless."

I have observed that girls who grow up in a fatherless environment are prone to be more sexually promiscuous. The women who worked alongside us in the juvenile detention centers reported that this was the most-discussed issue as they ministered to the girls. They were so hungry to talk with our ladies about being a woman and all that entailed.

Gangs in the major metropolitan cities are on the rise; jails, detention centers, and prisons are woefully crowded, with additional units being built. Death rows are full of men and women. Drug and alcohol abuse among teens is a constant source of escape for the pain these young people have to endure. All of this is a sign of the continual decay of family values and lack of parental care, especially from fathers. Sadly, there are political forces aggressively promoting agendas to further undermine the traditional family.

The advancement of the homosexual agenda, fueled by Hollywood and the entertainment industry, embraced by politicians at every level for votes and contributions, cuts at the very core of the family. God is very clear in His Scripture. In Romans 1:22–28 NASB, He addresses what we are seeing today. Excerpts from this are:

> "They exchanged the truth of God for a lie … for this reason God gave them over to degrading passions; for their women exchanged the natural function for that which is unnatural and in the same way also the men abandoned the natural function of the woman and burned in their desire towards one another, men with men committing indecent acts and receiving in their own persons the due penalty of their error."

Many other factors are coming to bear on the family. All seem to be bringing abject poverty—economically, emotionally, and spiritually—on the next generation. These forces, while most are well meaning, are inherently destructive. They have detached the father from the family in many ways. God's pattern for the family beginning in early Genesis has been usurped by man-made solutions with no hope of succeeding. Truth has been replaced by "relativity," and the wonderful experience of the trials and joys of marriage has given way to convenience and political correctness. God said in creation, "Let us make man in our image" (Genesis 1:26 KJV).

The image has become marred to the point that we cannot even recognize the innate attributes that went along with that pronouncement.

We have looked elsewhere for our answers, and quite frankly, they just don't work, nor will they ever. God speaks through Paul in 2 Timothy 3:16–17 NASB. He says, "All Scripture is inspired by God and profitable for teaching, for reproof, for correction, for training in righteousness; so that the man of God may be adequate, equipped for every good work." Teaching, reproof, correction, training—do you see and hear this? These are all the things necessary for being an adequate father. We simply have for several decades looked in the wrong places for direction and answers. Neither society nor government, unto themselves, are up to the task. Both, apart from God's holy guidance, lead to ruin. And that is where we find the family today, for the most part.

But there is always hope. The tide of decaying family life can be reversed and the values recaptured. But it will have to start, in my opinion, with men. Yes, men—current and would-be fathers. We must stop looking for fulfillment in our pursuit of pleasures and wealth or relying on a government program to provide the answer to our problem or dreams. True fulfillment will only come when men reassume their God-given roles in the home and take responsibility for its health and welfare.

When God said that He would "make man in His image," He meant just that. And He did not ill-equip us for the task. Why would He? What He entrusted us with is Himself. That is simply what Creators do. *"I will never leave you nor ever forsake you,"* is a profound promise found in Hebrews 13:5 NKJV.

Do you think Henry Ford, engineer of the late 1800s, would have abandoned his precious creation, the internal combustible engine? No? I agree. He nurtured it and turned it into an automotive and financial empire. And if Mr. Ford did, then why can we not trust that God would also? Men, we just have to start over and begin by looking at who we are and whose we are. The places from which anyone must proceed are *repentance and trust!* A much-quoted and trustworthy commandment and promise in the Bible is 2 Chronicles 7:13–14 NASB. God was challenging a wayward people to do what we must do. Place yourself in these verses as a man who desperately wants to be an *"abiding and adequate"* father to his children. You may find your marriage is suffering or you are failing in many ways as a father. Listen and heed these words.

> *If I shut up the heavens so there is no rain, or if I command the locust to devour the land, or if I send pestilence among My people, and My people who are called by My name humble themselves and pray, and seek My face and turn from their wicked ways, then I will hear from heaven, will forgive their sin, and will heal their land.*

The "land" of our families is in desperate need of that promise and help. Drought and pestilence are wreaking havoc. But it all begins with you and me. Do you care enough about your children and their future well-being to do this? One by one, we can turn this around. Don't wait for the next guy. Do it now. And watch God start delivering on His part of the bargain. You simply cannot go wrong. Will it be easy? *No!* Will it be worth it? *Yes!*

And if some of you are not sure if this applies to you, first go to the back of this book and redefine your relationship with the Living God. Maybe that is where many of us need to start.

MY FATHER

Chester Arthur Dotson (March 12, 1915–March 18, 1972) was my father. He died at the age of fifty-seven, way too young. He was the son of Floyd and Maude (Smith) Dotson and was the oldest boy of eight siblings. Born during the WWI era, he grew up as a young man during the Great Depression that followed. They were a farming family, and Pa Dotson was a successful businessman. He owned the country store and a cotton gin in Lawrence County, Tennessee. Dad, as I called him, received an eighth-grade education in a one-room country school with one teacher. Church is something the family attended on Sundays during the time of "all day singing and dinner on the ground." The horse and buggy was prevalent, as the automobile was just being developed. He learned to work, as did all the kids, at an early age, and this was prevalent throughout his life.

My earliest memory of him was around four years old. I had been born in Leoma, and Dad was given the responsibility to run his family sawmill in Franklin. He was already there, sixty miles away, when I was born during a six-inch snowstorm (in a house, no doctor, just mother and a friend who acted as the midwife). His dad died at age fifty-one with diabetes and from a heart attack. Soon thereafter, WWII broke out, and he and many of his friends enlisted. They were used to hard work, so they chose the navy and specifically the SeaBees (construction battalion). He once told me that not to believe the stories that the marines always landed first. The SeaBees, according to him, were there way before them, making it possible for the marines to come in. Dad was the child who inherited his mother's gift of cooking. So, since he liked it, he chose to be in the kitchen cooking for the men. This later served him well for the rest of his life. Most of his war service was in the small islands of Japan. He never shared much about his experiences, except he did say that the typhoons on Tinian were brutal. I observed later that anytime a storm arose, he would get up out of bed and walk throughout the house. He was a man who never feared much of anything, but I think those memories never left him.

Of course, I was very proud of my dad for being a serviceman. Most news of the war came through the movie theaters, although we would occasionally get a letter. I was about eight when one night I awakened to find him in bed with me. That was one of the most joyous times of my young life. Dad, my hero, was alive and home. He never again left. It was for the most part the beginning of my life with him. It was now post-Depression, post–war, and life in general was starting to get back to normal.

Mother, like most non-military women, had kept the home fire burning. She worked and supported us along with the meager pay from the navy. Once home, Dad searched for work wherever he could find it. The saw mill was gone, so it was up to him to find a job. After a few short years, he and Mother saw an opportunity to open a restaurant in Franklin with his uncle and aunt. And thus began a lifetime in the restaurant business. Dad's natural gift of cooking and his experience in the navy preparing for larger groups was the foundation of the business, which still exists under their name today. The first place was the Snack Shop. My dad ran the kitchen, and Mother ran the front. Their reputation grew quickly, as Dad's cooking was excellent. What I saw in this hard-working, barely educated man was a perfectionist. It had to be just right, and it had to be his way. He tried to teach me the art, but it died here. Never have I tasted fried chicken, catfish, cornbread, hushpuppies, or vegetables to equal his. He loved the compliments, and there was nothing he would not do to please his friends and customers through his giftedness. I often think about the expression, "Do you love to do something you enjoy or enjoy doing something you love?" I'm not sure of the answer, but that described Dad in his world.

Our youngest daughter, Evelyn, is a lot like him in certain ways. Maybe that led her partly to her current career. After earning a law degree, she moved into the food industry, getting a culinary degree and is presently a deputy editor with Martha Stewart. Being a health-conscious person and mom, she would never prepare and serve my dad's recipes, but she certainly has his gifts with food preparation.

Later on, Mother and Dad moved the restaurant around the corner into an antebellum building and named it Colonial Restaurant. That was the time I remember most, as I was a teenager by then. Much later, they moved again about a block away and opened Dotson's Restaurant that remains today under new ownership but same name—and reputation. Once Dad died in 1972, Mother continued the operation until she sold it. Earlier, they tried moving to Florida to join most of his siblings. They opened a restaurant in Auburndale and left the Franklin one under the management of a trusted employee. Due to mismanagement, they had to close the Florida one inside a year and move back to save Dotson's. Dad handled it reasonably well, although there was great disappointment in their associate and that their lives were rearranged from what they had hoped. They never again relinquished the management. Franklin was blessed to have them back. Some said the food suffered during Dad's absence.

To carry this further, whenever he would come to visit us in Dallas after Joanne and I moved, every morning we would awaken to cooking odors in the house. Always being an early, I mean 4:00 AM early, riser, he was in the kitchen preparing something to eat for the day.

Having grown up on a farm, he hunted and fished for food. There was no catch and release in the Depression. This also shaped him for life. He simply loved both. Eventually he and Mother bought a camp on Kentucky Lake. They loved the experience. He was truly at home there. That is where he died during the night in his sleep from a heart attack with a family member. Being a man's man, and a great chef, whatever he shot or caught was field dressed or filleted. And eventually it reached the skillet.

He really worked at trying to get his only child to embrace the hunting and fishing. We spent quite a bit of time doing that early on, and it was great. He was quietly teaching me his world. As I have told him and many more, he would be catching fish but not me; we would trade places and he would catch and not me; we would switch poles and he would catch and not me. He really tried. I really failed.

As a young child, our oldest daughter, Becky, loved to go fishing with him. He and she got great pleasure from that. Even today, she still loves fishing and so do her kids. She even married a fisherman. One experience I will never forget. She, Dad, and I were trolling one early morning. I had noticed a water moccasin swimming alongside the boat. He disappeared from view, and I quickly forgot about it. We had pulled our outboard motor out of the water so we could troll with the electric motor. It was a sunny morning and very peaceful, until Dad suggested we drop the motor and go around the bend. I was driving, so I leaned over and grabbed the bar to lower the motor when my hand contacted the snake, who had wrapped himself around the motor to warm in the sunshine. Being a person who has always feared snakes, I did what any scared man would do. I jumped back, and with that we saw the snake slither into the boat. I grabbed my daughter and we got on one of the far-away benches. I did consider jumping into the lake for one split moment. Not my dad. After looking at his wimpy son, he proceeded to attack the problem. He convinced me to help, and together we trapped the enemy and tossed him back into the lake. As a father, this was not a proud moment for me. But that was my dad.

While hunting as a child, he would teach me the ways of caring for the guns, safety, and the skill of hunting. He always had a lot of guns and pistols. We hunted rabbits, squirrels, and birds. And at times we shot rattlers and copperhead snakes. Again, he was a good shot and I was so-so. There was one character trait I learned from him one early morning. When squirrel hunting, we always arrived before daylight; maybe that is what I did not like—getting up so early. This allowed us to be in place when they came out of their nests without scaring them away. One morning in particular stands out. We used rifles, as Dad said it was not fair to hunt them with a shotgun. I looked up and aimed to shoot into the nest, as they would be "sitting ducks." That is when I learned something more about his character. He stopped me and informed me this was not sporting. That would be murder, plus the fact the babies might get killed. I never forgot that.

Being in the restaurant business, Dad had a lot of friends, primarily those with whom he hunted. Deer season was always special for them. He would always invite me, but I never went, much to his disappointment I am sure. I told him I had seen *Bambi* too many times to ever shoot a deer. His buddies knew how well my dad could prepare their meats, so he was always the one cooking for them after any type hunt. The restaurant was their go-to place, and Chester was their go-to man.

I never heard my dad ever say the words, "I love you" or that he was proud of me. But so many people would tell me how much he bragged on me to them. That was very affirming to me. Nor did he spend time addressing the more serious issues of life. But I did learn from him as I observed his good and bad actions. As most men in that era, he smoked probably two to three packs of cigarettes a day. He loved his bourbon and beer. But I never once saw him drunk. He seemed to be able to hold his liquor. Cursing was a part of his dialogue, and yet he seemed to always tone it way down around me and my family. I never cursed in front of him, although I had learned the language early on. I did not want to encourage him in this area, and for the most part I was ashamed for him and me.

Dad was always there for Mother and me. I never had the fear he would leave us. That was very comforting. He was honest, hard working, and had an aversion to debt, similar to most Depression families. He had excellent credit and was well-thought of in the community. He was not a business leader, but he served wherever he was asked or needed. During the early years of their business, around 1950, we had a major snow and ice storm that disrupted many lives for several weeks, including eventual flooding. People were without ways to cook, and food was short. My parents did not miss a beat in serving their customers. They cooked with gas and were one of the few places where people could eat. At the time we lived in Arno, about ten miles from town. They never missed opening the restaurant, and they fed all who came. Many did not have the funds to pay, but that never stopped them from serving them. People in Franklin never forgot that, nor did I.

Dad loved Joanne and his granddaughters. You just saw it in his eyes and the way he loved playing with them. Sadly, just about the time they were getting to an age where he could have done more things with them, he died. Becky was twelve, and Evelyn was eight. And for me, I think I missed out on a lot by not having him in my life for the past thirty years. He was not an openly affectionate man, but he was passionate for life. Not being very religious, he, like many, usually attended church Christmas and Easter. That was special to me to see him dressed up and being there. I, for the most part, was sent to church, as they worked seven days a week most years until later life. Interestingly, he was musically inclined, as I saw him occasionally playing the piano or organ by ear. His favorite hymn was "How Great Thou Art." That seemed to comfort me, as I believed there was some spiritual life in him. About a year before his death, my life took a significant turn. I wrote a letter to Mother and Dad about what I call a "born-again" experience. Mother told me she fell to her knees and rededicated her life to the Lord. Shortly thereafter, I learned to share the gospel. I became heavily burdened to share the good news with Dad. After much prayer and hesitation, I got the chance to be alone with him one afternoon. It was difficult for me, but I presented the gospel to him as clearly as I could and asked him to consider trusting Christ also if he had never done so. We ended the time without any action on his part but saying he understood. Only a few months later, we received the call that he had died in his sleep.

Naturally, my thoughts were centered mostly on his salvation. While at his funeral, Mother said one of his cooks wanted to speak to me about Chester. We visited, and she seemed to be confident that something had taken place in his life over the past few months. He had told her, a believer, that Billy (me) had talked to him recently and that he had been thinking about a lot of things and he felt he needed to start going to church. She was convinced Chester was in heaven, that change had taken place in his heart. Only eternity will reveal the truth, but it is at least comforting to know someone saw something in him during those last days that gave her and me hope.

While Dad was trying to spend time with me through hunting and fishing, I was becoming involved in competitive sports. This was not his world. He attended only a game or two over my school years because of work. I understood, but there was a void in me by him not being there. This shaped my future life with my children and now grandchildren. One interesting moment stands out to me. I was quite fast for short distances. One day I came home, showing my medal, as I had won a sprint in track. He joked with me that he could outrun me, even at his age. I accepted the challenge, as there was no way that my middle-aged dad who smoked and was overweight would have a chance. I think I was thirteen. We marked off the distance. He even ran in his long pants and work shoes. I was in shorts and tennis shoes. On your mark, get set, go! I got the early jump, but he passed me and never looked back. He admitted later that if it had been ten yards farther, he would have died. I did notice the deep gasps for breath. But there was no way he was going to let me win. I gained a lot of respect for his competitive nature that day. We never raced again.

I had joined the Scouts early on. We had a banquet for fathers and sons. Lo and behold, Dad wanted to go and took off work. It was very crowded, and just about the time the meal was to start, one last father and son came in the back. Dad looked around and saw that there were no seats left. Without hesitation, he got up, went over to them, and gave the boy his seat. He stood with the other father the whole time and never ate. I was the proudest boy there. He had said to me as he was getting up that he could eat later at home. That showed me a lot about his heart.

He always let me know that Joanne was his choice for me. Our wedding plans went out to friends and family. Dad was my best man—and he let me know that if he was present, he would definitely be the best man there. Ninety percent of the time he was dressed in a T-shirt and work pants or hunting or fishing clothes. I sorta worried how he would handle the formal wear of a tuxedo. It was his first ever. But he pulled it off well. That was the last time, though. He looked so handsome, and I was very proud to be his son. (Oh, on the day of the wedding, he took me out in the country to shoot cans and bottles on fence posts with his pistols. I told you he loved hunting!)

Another act on his part is worth repeating. Dad loved new cars, and he saved up and paid cash always. Most everyone then was a one-car family. Joanne and I were going to Miami to a real estate conference. He heard about it, and as I recall, a few days before leaving to drive, we were in the front yard of our first home. A gold Cadillac Eldorado convertible, fins and all, came down the street, and Dad was driving it. He had bought it in time for us to drive it to Miami on our trip. How many people do you know that would lend their brand new Cadillac to their young son and trust him to bring it back undamaged after a two thousand-mile trip? That simply was my dad. He got great joy out of surprises and pleasing others.

There were some other minor remembrances in which Dad was involved: my first BB gun as a kid, a 410 gauge shotgun at twelve; him making a wooden sled one morning from scratch during the ice storm I mentioned and being pulled behind the Model-T throughout the countryside; after being awakened by a neighbor's horn, he carried me from our house during late evening through three feet of water while it was flooding during that same year; our first Dumont TV that he wanted so much; all the puppies and dogs he got me; the dyed Easter duck named Junior; my pet squirrel he caught and caged; his warning me to not put my finger in the cage, as they have sharp teeth; yes, I did anyway, and yes they do; he was a safe and careful driver; he taught me and many other family members to drive; he never once spanked me; every one of Mother's large family loved him, and he seemed to be one of the favorites; his laughter—he loved joking; working with his hands and making things from wood; giving me a pocket knife and teaching me to whittle; love for his El Camino in his later years; treating people fairly; and once more—all the great food!

My hope is that my earthly father is now residing with my Heavenly Father and that he is cooking up something special for the King!

Questions to Ponder

What would be in your short review on your father?

Would it be worth setting out the thoughts on paper?

Do you think your children and grandchildren would benefit from reading it?

What's holding you back?

CHAPTER 1: ABSENT

AWOL: *Absent without Official Leave*
—U. S. Military

"Absent without leave," meaning absent without permission, is of a military origin. This has a long history in the British navy and army. The rules at the time, as early as the 1700s, were that a sailor was deemed to have deserted if he missed three roll calls. AWOL was of U. S. military origin. Some suggest this came much later than "absent without leave," probably just prior to WWII. But there is also some unsubstantiated evidence of it being used in the American Civil War. M. L. Menchen, in *The American Language, 1945* states: "(In the Confederate Army) absences of short duration were often unpunished and in other cases offenders received such trivial sentences as reprimand by a company officer, digging a stump, carrying a rail for an hour or two, wearing a placard inscribed with the letters AWOL."[10] I suggest, in the case of absent fathers, that the placard might still be appropriate, at a minimum.

Webster would tell us that "absent" means, "*Not being in a specified place physically or mentally.*"[1] Let's address the physical aspects of absenteeism—as a child, being absent from school and then as an adult, being absent from work. There are excused absences, like when you are sick, or having to go to the dentist and your parent writes an "excuse my kid" note. Or one calls in sick with the flu or short-term sicknesses.

Most employers have certain designated number of days you may miss without losing pay. Some employees even "milk the system" to maximize the benefit. I bet most of us have turned up sick as a child on the day of the big test that we have not studied for, hoping for leniency and more time to prepare. All of these and similar examples are reasonably acceptable by society in most instances.

But what about the numerous absences, going well beyond reasonable? The work product is suffering; the student is getting way too far behind to ever catch up. This starts exhibiting "chronic" behavior, indicating a habit of long standing, possibly being permanent. Absenteeism costs the employers in America billions of dollars every year in expenses and missed revenue, not counting faulty products or reduced services. Sooner than later, this has to be dealt with. Some means to deal with this are leaves of absence without pay all the way to termination. In school, discipline ranges from detention or demerits that have to be served to possible expulsion. The schools and local authorities spend valuable time and money to police "truancy," primarily in our public schools.

Then there is the mental side of absenteeism. The student sits through a class but the mind is somewhere else. Thoughts other than the subject matter cloud the brain. The neat date this Friday night, the ballgame coming up, daydreaming about the summer vacation—all these and many more cloud the mind. The child is present but at the same time absent. He or she is not participating in an activity that someday would pay dividends if he or she had only been engaged.

It is the same at work. Problems with the boss or at home, bills piling up, lack of sleep, pondering a job change, and figuring ways to beat the system can cause an employee to be mentally absent. Yes, the employee showed up for work and is physically there, but mentally and emotionally, he or she is elsewhere. And when the review comes and it's not favorable, the employee wonders why the boss would do this to him or her, such a faithful employee who is always at the job. Just maybe the results of the work production reflect the mental absenteeism.

The same is true for fathers; they can be absent physically, emotionally, or mentally. There are many uncontrollable reasons for physical absence. Death, hospitalization, armed services, or an extended mission are some. These have to be dealt with, and they must be addressed to secure the best outcome possible. But the reasons that seem to ravage a home range from broken marriages ending in separation or divorce all the way to assuming job positions that require extended travel or exorbitant work hours that force separation from the family unit.

If you will allow, I'll share a personal experience in my life. Like any red-blooded American man, I was seeking to climb the ladder and provide for my ego—oops, family. An offer to move from Nashville to Dallas (a bigger pond) came, and I took it without consulting my family. But that is another story. With the new opportunity came the requirement that I travel extensively during the week, with some over-the-weekend junkets. Mind you, I was doing this and making the "sacrifice" for "them." It was just part of the territory with this public multi-state apartment developer. See, I was executive vice president, and I had to find and approve all sites, plus arrange the financing for each project. This was a big, important job, and I wanted to succeed, or at least not fail. And at the time, Dallas was a poor market, so we went elsewhere every week, it seemed.

After a while, I sensed that my seven- and ten-year-old children were going to be grown and gone and I would not know them, or they me. My wife did not complain. She was a great mother and understanding wife. But the unrest inside me drove me to resign and start my own development firm. Financially, it was a bad decision. It was during the Carter administration when prime rate went to 20+ percent. My income suffered (two years without any), but by God's grace, we survived. Most importantly, I was in the home again, engaged. The girls would have to tell their side of the story. They may have gotten more of me than they wanted. Would I do it again? Absolutely! It may have been the most creative time in our family as we stretched everything and saw God provide continually, but not without problems and hardships. Personally, I have never grown spiritually more than I did during those lean years. He never said parenting was going to be easy, only worthwhile.

If your circumstances require uncontrollable absence from the home for a period of time, there are ways to be creative and still be the father your children need. They will see your desire to be there for them and sense your love. Your wife will provide the means to be productive in their lives. They are simply built that way. Trust them to assist in your "fathering from afar."

I grew up an only child in a small town in Tennessee. It was post-Depression and WWII. After my dad came home from service, much to my joy, they, like 90+ percent of Americans, had to knuckle down and make a living in rather lean times. I understood and appreciated my parents' dedication. They worked six and sometimes seven days a week in their restaurant operation. But as I grew and started playing sports, I really missed their not ever being there and sensing their support. I think that is why I made the decision in Dallas to make sure I never missed anything in which our daughters were participating. We still attend every grandchild event possible. Dad tried to make up for it in hunting and fishing, as that is who he was. Being physically present is very important. Never underestimate its positive impact.

I have watched the recent movie *Facing the Giants* a few times with the grandkids. There are many great life lessons in the movie, but one stands out in my mind. David, a small-framed soccer player, is encouraged to try out for the football team.

His dad, a man confined to a life in a wheelchair, encourages him to try. It doesn't go that well, as he really does not have a strong leg. But in a critical final series of a championship game, the coach makes a decision to send David in to win the game with a field goal. It was from a long distance, farther than he had ever kicked. As he approaches the position, he looks down the field and sees his father out of his wheelchair standing on his own legs with his arms stretched skyward as if to say, "I believe in you, and it will be good." The ball is snapped, and he kicks so hard that he falls down; the ball sails through the air and then between the goal posts. Good! Who do you think made it possible for David to make that field goal, which was well outside his range? That is simply what fathers do. Equip their children to do far greater things than they could ever imagine.

Well, this father was both physically and mentally present. But what about you? You're at home, but you are mentally elsewhere. Do you believe that is possible? Examine your routine when you arrive home at whatever time. Are you rushing to give a hug or high five and inquire about your children's day? Or is it the newspaper first? "Well, I have worked all day, and I need my quiet time to catch up on the news." Maybe it is with a beer or drink. "I really need to relax." The kids honor your space but desire to be engaged. Modern man may be on the phone or texting when he arrives and the work day is still not over. Important jobs require you be available 24/7. Dad thinks or explains that it puts food on the table and clothes on their back. Meanwhile, communication inside the family is desperately suffering. "Right after dinner, guys; I need to finish the work I brought home. A big client dropped this on us today." "But Dad, don't you remember? I have a scout meeting tonight and you promised you would be there." Little sis pipes in, "Yeah, and you were going to help me on my work project for school tonight. It is due tomorrow, and you have said all week we would finish it." You get the picture of many

American homes. A Scripture (Eph. 6:4a NASB) comes to mind here, "Fathers, do not provoke your children to anger."

And lest we forget the all-American god—television. "What, honey? Just a minute, I don't want to miss this play." "Dad, from the time you get home, you flip on the sports and we never get to throw ball or work on my class projects together." "Well, we can start watching this together if you like. Son, how is your team doing this year?" "Dad, I dropped off the team, as I am no good." "What? My boy not playing sports? I'll have a talk with the coach. We'll get this straightened out." "Did you not hear me? I quit on my own. I told you I was and you weren't listening, like always."

Hellllo, is there anyone home? Maybe you are physically but not mentally or emotionally. Can you imagine the frustration that starts building up in your children when they want so badly to be recognized and listened to by you? You are the one person from whom they draw a mental image of God. Most have no one else to engage. You are the head of the house, from a leadership standpoint. They are seeking and greatly need your attention and input. They are trying to grow up the best way they know how. You are supposed to be older and wiser, the person they can turn to for counsel. Families function best when this is happening. But when it doesn't, a myriad of bad scenarios start developing. *"Listen* to me, Dad. I am a person, your responsibility. I am struggling with choices. I need answers—from you!"

Sadly, most men have never been equipped to take on the role of father/parent. Possibly, their role model dad was similar to them. Fruit never falls too far from the tree. Bad fathering breeds more bad fathering and so on. It is easier to get immersed in most anything else and leave the parenting to the mother, near relatives, teachers, and coaches. Some even believe that since he made it through tough times, so can his kids. A few bumps and bruises never hurt anyone. They are good kids; they'll make it. But will they, and if they do, would they have been far better equipped if their father, *you*, had fulfilled their role as designed by the Heavenly Father? It is no accident or TV gimmickry that virtually every athlete looking into the sideline camera mouths the words, "Hi, Mom!" Maybe, just maybe, they don't "know" the dad in their life.

One of the most vivid examples of the "absence" factor of fathers was during a session with twenty-four young boys from eleven to seventeen years of age in the Dallas County Juvenile Detention Center several years ago. Our assignment was to share thoughts on the word "revere." I explained simply that it meant honoring or showing respect for someone. Then I asked the boys to list all the people they thought should be revered. To get them engaged and participating, I always rewarded them with a small piece of candy for any attempt to answer a question. So, up went the hands, and out came the answers. Mothers, aunts, grandmothers, firemen, police (reluctantly), judges, the president, teachers, and pastors. Maybe twenty or so names surfaced the first time around. I asked them to dig deeper and think of more. A few more names came to their mind, like doctors and nurses. Then silence. I challenged them with two pieces of candy for the one name missing from the list. Still silence.

Can you picture this? Twenty-four bright boys and ten minutes have passed. And they are studying all the names on the board. I started to spell, and after the "f," a boy shouted father. He was hungry. At this, I stated to them, "Boys, do you realize you did not even think of your dad as one you should honor?" The fact is, fathers were just not significant in most of their lives. I was so overcome by this lack of presence or influence. At this, I asked a few questions about how many lived with, or even knew, their fathers. Three or four had a father in their lives at some level. One of them was the boy who answered the last question. Coincidental? I think not. That morning has stuck in my mind more than any other over the ten years of teaching at the JDC. Fact: their fathers were just not a part of their world. Frightening—and very sad.

For most of you, it is never, ever too late to change what has happened previously. It takes an honest evaluation of who you are, what your role really is, and where you need to start. For some, it is going to be heart wrenching. Others will find you have not strayed too far away for a quick reversal. My observation is that the children have been waiting for this day all their lives. Strangely, they get it, this parenting stuff. They always have. Why have most fathers been so blinded to the same truth? We'll examine this and so much more in the next chapters. Are you ready to go farther with us? It only requires that you turn the pages, one at a time. But before you do, read the words to this wonderful, maybe sad, song by the deceased Harry Chapin entitled *Cat's in the Cradle.*

A child arrived just the other day,
He came to the world in the usual way.
But there were planes to catch, and bills to pay.
He learned to walk while I was away.
And he was talking 'fore I knew it, and as he grew,
He'd say, "I'm gonna be like you, dad.
You know I'm gonna be like you."

And the cat's in the cradle and the silver spoon,
Little boy blue and the man in the moon.
"When you coming home, dad?" "I don't know when,
But we'll get together then.
You know we'll have a good time then."

My son turned ten the other day.
He said, "Thanks for the ball, dad, come on let's play.
Can you teach me to throw?" I said, "Not today,
I got a lot to do." He said, "That's ok."
And he walked away, but his smile never dimmed,
Said, "I'm gonna be like him, yeah.
You know I'm gonna be like him."

And the cat's in the cradle and the silver spoon,
Little boy blue and the man in the moon.
"When you coming home, dad?" "I don't know when,
But we'll get together then.
You know we'll have a good time then."

Well, he came from college just the other day,
So much like a man I just had to say,
"Son, I'm proud of you. Can we sit for a while?"
He shook his head, and he said with a smile,
"What I'd really like, dad, is to borrow the car keys.
See you later. Can I have them please?"

And the cat's in the cradle and the silver spoon,
Little boy blue and the man in the moon.
"When you coming home, son?" "I don't know when,
But we'll get together then.
You know we'll have a good time then."

I've long since retired and my son's moved away.
I called him up just the other day.
I said, "I'd like to see you if you don't mind."
He said, "I'd love to, dad, if I could find the time.
You see, my new job's a hassle, and the kid's got the flu.
But it's sure nice talking to you, dad.
It's been sure nice talking to you."
And as I hung up the phone, it occurred to me,
He'd grown up just like me.
My boy was just like me.

And the cat's in the cradle and the silver spoon,
Little boy blue and the man in the moon.
"When you coming home, son?" "I don't know when,
But we'll get together then, dad.
You know we'll have a good time then."[12]

If you see yourself anywhere in this tune, it is time to take action, start addressing the changes needed, and there is never a better time than the present.

Questions to Ponder

Are you an absentee father, physically, mentally, emotionally, or all three?

If, so, how do you think it is affecting your children?

Do you want to become re-engaged with them?

How will you go about this?

CHAPTER 2: ABIDING

A journey of a thousand miles begins with a single step.[13]
—Lao-Tzu

Some mysteries or novels leave the end for the last chapter. Since I am not a professional author, I thought you might like to know where we are headed and the desired result. This will keep you from having to skim to the back and possibly not even have to read the entire book. You get no money back if you skip the hard part.

Also, there is no "real zinger" to work up to after numerous chapters. In fact, you can read this book in any order you prefer. And for you not-so-well-organized minds, this should be real freedom. And I decided to not charge more for that privilege. Maybe I should have chosen Random House as the publisher. Sorta fitting, don't you think?

But truly, this is how so many fathers conduct their parenting. No plan! Get 'em out of diapers, into real clothes, through school and maybe college, grab a good job, hope they meet someone you like and marry them, choose the right political party, and if you're lucky, there will be grandchildren at the end. Who said there was no plan?

But the truth is, most credit falls on the wife and mother for the majority of modern American families. And if she has a career outside the home also, the kids are sacrificed. I know, certain financially strapped parents just can't do it any other way. I would dare to say that many fathers place their families in the "strapped" condition with too many toys, keeping up with the Joneses, and insurmountable debt.

So, what we have in these families is a non-resident/absent mom and dad, which is even worse for the development of their children. But there are choices we can make, hopefully early on, that will lessen the load along the way. Children are very flexible, and if involved and made aware, they can be very constructive contributors to the health of the family.

So, where are we headed? What is the end result fathers should plan for and pursue? Simple—fathers *abiding* in the home. Fathers should be going *from faith to faith*! Fathers need to go from being *absent* in the home to *abiding* in the home. See, it's that simple. Piece of cake! But first, you have to want this—*really* want this. Because once this course of action becomes your overriding objective, many changes will need to take place. In some cases, they will be drastic, while others will be less of a chore.

Now, I am at this point assuming you believe this is a worthy cause: your family's current health and well-being and the foundation for future generations to come. Sacrifices at most levels will be required. Priorities will have to change. You'll have to make plans—yuck!—and seek the help and approval of your family, immediate and extended, possibly. Does the end justify the means? You bet. But it is your conscious decision that is most important.

Okay, Bill, what does this new me look like in a nutshell? Paint me the ideal picture, but first, what does the word "abiding" mean? Good question. Glad you asked, because for some, if not most of you, it is new terminology. Let's start in *Webster's Dictionary* and move from there. I think it will start becoming clear what it is to look like but how to get there won't. That's why this book contains a lot more than two chapters.

Abiding is an adjective and basically means "unceasing," like an abiding belief or faith. Some other really definitive word pictures are: certain, changeless, constant, durable, enduring, immovable, firm, reliable, steadfast, and unfaltering, to name a few. The word appears in the Greek Bible as far back as 250 bc. In John 5:38 NASB, Jesus spoke these words: "You do not have His word abiding in you, for you do not believe Him whom He sent."

It says to me, "dwelling constantly."

The verb *abide* does mean to dwell or reside. A few synonyms are: acknowledge, stay, remain, stand, suffer, support, and tolerate.[14] I like this contextual picture as it relates to the presence of someone or something: inhabit, live, lodge, perch, or take up one's abode. As it relates to perseverance, there is an expression I have heard and used often, "Keep on keeping on." Daniel Webster was quoted as saying, "If we abide by the principles taught by the Bible, our country will go on prospering."[15] If I may take the liberty of changing one word, it might bring home a strong point for us to ponder. What if we substituted "family" in place of "country"? Considering that a country is made up of families, maybe Daniel was on to something that works for both.

Even if you are not a student of the Bible, it would be worth exploring chapter 15 in the gospel of John. The word abide appears thirteen times in ten verses. The picture is of a vine and a branch being connected, abiding together and being productive for their intended purpose. Think with me. If in a family, the vine represents the father, and the branches are the children; if the two are separated for whatever reason, one can easily see the disastrous results. The branches die for loss of the lifeline. They become starved for the sustenance they need to survive and grow into a fruitful person.

So, now that we have a little better idea of this "abiding" thing, what should you and I as fathers take from this? Please know that when I speak of the children, this involves the wife and mother. Best fathers involve their wives, the kids' mother, in it all.

We have to be present.

We have to be engaged.

We have to be attentive.

We have to be willing to suffer with and for our children.

We have to support our children.

We have to be consistent.

We have to be there for the long run.

We have to be firm, unfaltering—coupled with compassion.

We have to be reliable.

We have to be their best role model.

Now, that wasn't too hard, was it? These ten items are only a nutshell of the full requirements of being an abiding father. And I dare say if most of us were hitting on all cylinders as defined above, we would, ourselves, be the most joyous group of men on the face of the earth. We need to know that even with the best "how-to" manual, none of us are going to come out perfectly. As in many things worth doing, it is not so much the grade as it is the pursuit. And in the pursuit to be the "best abiding father" you can be, you'll find that even when you fall short, there will be fulfillment in the attempt. And when the children see you trying, it is easier for them to forgive you, and I bet they will even be there to pick you up. Why? Because they sense you really do care for them, even when you blow it. And we all do.

For those who have now got it all figured out and don't want to read the rest of the book, please pass it on to someone you know who does not. You won't have to look far. They are all around us. As for you who think there might be some meat left on this bone, and since you paid for the darn thing (or your wife and children did), you might as well finish it; I hope you do, because you want to maybe find ways to become the greatest father in the whole wide world to your kids. Your wife, their mother, for one, will be a blessed woman. Let's explore the world of moving from *absent* to *abiding,* remembering the first step is always the hardest.

Questions to Ponder

Do you desire to be an abiding father?

What will it require on your part?

What results would you wish to see?

CHAPTER 3: UNDERSTANDING THE ROLE

Seek the wisdom of the ages, but look at the world through the eyes of a child.[16]

We simply cannot avoid the fact that there are males and there are females—man/woman, boy/girl, both human, both unique. When God created humankind, He declared it "very good." He first of all made man from the dust of the earth; He shaped him and formed him. Then He drew woman from the body of the first man when he was placed into a deep sleep. God brought the partner, not yet named, to Adam. He declared, "This is now bone of my bones, and flesh of my flesh; she shall be called Woman, because she has been taken out of Man" (Gen 2:23 NKJV). That is why two people who marry leave and cleave. They *leave* the dominion of the parents and *cleave* to one another, becoming *"one flesh."* They are equal in the eyes of God but have clearly distinctive roles.

When both are fulfilling their roles, the other is enhanced. As children are introduced into the family by natural birth or adoption, these two become no longer just husband and wife; they are now also father and mother. They are still equal but clearly different in responsibility. Certain societies and cultures treat this slightly differently, but clearly, from a standpoint of father and mother, these roles are not to be reversed. As I was reading Deuteronomy 22:5 NASB this week, I was intrigued by one of God's various laws for Israel. "A woman shall not wear man's clothing, nor shall a man put on a woman's clothing; for whoever does these things is an abomination to the Lord your God." It is not just a no-no but an abomination. "Who wears the pants in your house?" may have derived from this.

But if you are the one who has been appointed to "wear the pants" of fatherhood, don't you think you ought to know a little, hopefully a lot, about the responsibilities? When one applies for a job, the employer usually provides a list of the primary duties that accompany the position. Applicants usually present their resumes or bios, showing why they are qualified to be hired. For it to really be a great fit, the two should match up. But one must also expect that under a new employer, even though the employee is qualified, there will be expected adjustments. It is the same with fathering.

Let's examine some qualifications from our typical man. "Let's see: 1) I'm a healthy male; 2) I'm married; 3) I have a decent education; 4) I'm employed; 5) I played a little ball in school; 6) I like kids; and 7) my parents were good, church-going folks. Well, I guess that's about it. With time, I am sure I could think of more things." As a reader, how would you rate him? If you were assigning kids, would he rank high enough to get one or two? I admit, he sounds decent, but is he qualified to take on the role of leading a family with precious cargo, children? We simply don't know enough. But on the surface, there is not much meaningful evidence that would indicate he has a solid grip on fatherhood. Yes, having kids; but fathering them? Maybe, maybe not.

Do you think God goes through this scenario every time He decides to allow a man to become the father of one of His creations? He told the first parents to procreate: "Be fruitful and multiply and fill the earth and subdue it. . ." (Genesis 1:28 NASB).

That was the only stipulation, but later He gave many laws for living and the blessings that go along with obedience, and yes, the consequences of disobedience. He did not just throw us out into this place called Earth and let us free fall. There are laws of every nature that He set into play, and all are designed for our good. The manual for fatherhood can best be studied and understood when you know the Author personally.

Let us identify and examine what many would say are overriding critical elements in a good father.

1) Admit you are unqualified.
2) Seek help from role models.
3) Listen to your wife.
4) Pray a lot.

That's it. Case closed. You got it! Frankly speaking, that is all there is. We see humility, and boy, is it humbling. We see a man seeking good counsel and will he ever need it. He is man enough to ask for input from his equal, one flesh mate. And prayer engages the one who made you a man and has the power to help you finish the race well. I did not say perfectly; I said well.

Maybe you are similar to many of us men. Prior to navigation devices, this is how it might have gone if my family had a long trip to make. As the "man," I'm driving. I take a glance at a map; I get my general bearings in my mind. I fill the tank and secure the luggage, and the wife suggests we might take the map just in case. After some minor debate, I yield to the gal who will be riding "shotgun" just to pacify her. Then down the road, some extensive road work crops up. Detours are encountered. But I still have my bearings. No problem. It starts getting a little dark. I'm thinking to myself, *Seems like we'll never get back to the main road.* Then she asks the wrong question. "Honey, are we lost?" With that, the kids want to know, "Are we there yet?" We are fine; just a few more miles. And then comes the killer: "Honey, did you ever make those motel reservations we discussed last week? It had a pool for the kids, and we all are getting hungry. Sugar, do you think maybe, just maybe, you might stop and ask someone?" That did it! Question my manhood, will you?

Many of you have experienced this in some way. We fathers start out to be a parent with limited credentials or preparation, and when the derailments come, we are too proud to seek help or even listen to our mates. You ask, "What do they know about my role?" And at the same time, the kids are getting unruly and impatient with our lack of wisdom and leadership. It's time to stop the car. Get out, take a deep breath, and find directions. "Where there is no guidance, the people fall, but in abundance of counselors, there is victory" (Prov. 11:14 NASB).

Maybe some of you had ideal fathers and you received supreme counsel and direction on your journey as a father. But the rest of us stiffs learned it on the fly, by the seat of our pants. And one great divide, even to the best equipped, is the changing culture between each generation. "I will raise my kids the way I was raised" just won't get it most of the time. Believe me, I tried it. I grew up as a child in a small town. We raised our girls in the big city. Big difference! There were different strategies required.

Back to the role.

As a man, you have been appointed to assume the supreme leadership in the home.

With proper help, you are well equipped to assume this role.

This leadership involves all your troops (wife and kids), not just you.

You are the "spiritual" leader, the primary channel of wisdom and knowledge.

While discipline is for both parents, ultimately, it falls on the father.

Final decisions are ultimately your responsibility; the buck stops here!

You are to model your role in a manner that prospers the family.

You should continue to hone your skills as a father.

Empower your children; don't control them.

You must develop listening skills for constructive communication.

Invest yourself in your children.

Your eyes should be focused on the privilege you have to equip the next generation.

To accomplish this and more, you must be present and engaged. Informed, aware, and responsive fathers make the best choices and decisions. And if you were to sum up all of these following chapters together into a single word—it would be **discipleship!** The role is simply being a *disciple maker*.

None of the above can be handled by a heavy-handed, egotistical male chauvinist. It simply will fail, and miserably. But so many men use their size and position to demand respect rather than earning respect. In the long run, men, fathers, that is what we seek—*respect*. How we get it depends on the kind of father we are perceived to be, with the primary audience being our children. You simply cannot fool them. Don't even try. And remember, they are *your* kids, so they must be smart. In fact, you will find early on that they are smarter than you were at the same age.

Questions to Ponder

Do you have a more complete understanding of your role?

In what areas are you performing now?

In what areas do you need to begin or seek improvement?

Are you willing to make the effort?

CHAPTER 4: A'LOVING

Love never gives up.
Love cares for others more than self.
Love doesn't want what it doesn't have.
Love doesn't strut,
Doesn't have a swelled head,
Doesn't force itself on others, isn't always 'me first',
Doesn't fly off the handle,
Doesn't keep score of the sins of others,
Doesn't revel when others grovel,
Takes pleasure in the flowering of truth, puts up with
anything, trusts God always, always looks for the
best, never looks back, but keeps going to the end.

—Apostle Paul
1 Corinthians 13:4–7 (MSG)

Men, for you and me, this is "the" challenge. What an uphill struggle for most of us. The majority simply do not know how to love. Sadly, I dare say the words "I love you" are not even in us. Maybe they never reached your ears from your dad when growing up. My generation, for the most part, believed our fathers loved us, but we never heard it. Several years ago, I participated in a Bible study with men about my age. The discussion one day centered on this subject. Only one of the five had ever heard their father verbally say, "I love you." Would we have liked to hear it? Absolutely!

But see, we are all wrapped up in *respect* and not love as men. We give respect and hope to receive it. Love is a difficult but necessary attribute. "I knew my dad loved me, but he just never said it." How many times have I heard this over the years? Too much, that's for sure. So, if this is an oft-asked question, might we assume it is a "biggie" relative to fathering? Certainly, you can give lip service and never show love with your actions. I suggest it cannot be either/or but both/and.

The absolute model for us is found in a Bible verse familiar to most, John 3:16. "For God so loved … that He gave." And when Jesus was baptized, a special ceremony in anyone's life, a voice was heard by those present saying "This is My beloved Son, in whom I am well pleased." Would you not want to hear those words spoken over you anytime, anywhere? After saying this to His Son, three years later God sacrificed (gave) His Son on a cross for the remission of our sins. He not only spoke it, but He also demonstrated it. But you ask, "Why would a father sacrifice his son? That's not very loving; in fact, it is downright cruel and unloving." The answer to this very sound question is found also in the Scriptures. His Son's death had already been determined by Him and His Son to be the only means to show how much they loved us and redeem us from sin's judgment. And by believing (trusting) this, we too are adopted as sons of God. The Heavenly Father was demonstrating His love for us through His Son. And His final act of love to His Son here on earth was the resurrection, raising Him from the dead and seating Him at His right hand.

Now, you and I most likely will never be called to show our love in this way, by giving our life for our children. But this does happen, and there are many stories to confirm that. The point is that this was the ultimate in demonstrating love, both spoken and through action. This should be the model for us. God doesn't want or need our respect, and neither does His Son. Nor do our children. They want and need to hear (and see) that we love them, just like they are, not only after they "straighten up." Helping them with the straightening up is another matter altogether. That will take care of itself much easier when they know they are loved unconditionally. Jesus did not die for us after or if we would clean up our act but with full knowledge of our disobedience. Men, that is love! That is love that creates an atmosphere in which all can constructively face the issues of life in a family head on, together.

So, what really is love? We're not talking Hollywood love scenes nor brotherly love. And it isn't "I love Cajun food" or "I love my new car." These are expressions of affection for something that benefits you. Love is an emotion of the heart, and not of the palate.[17] We're talking about the expressions of word and deed that bring out the best in the object of that devotion with no hope or need for reward. What you say and do are simply for the interest of another and in the case of a father, your children.

Interestingly, the Scriptures record Jesus saying in John 14:15, 21 , "If you love Me, you will obey Me … and if you obey Me, you demonstrate that you love Me" (my paraphrase). This would tell us that love is not always emotional; in fact, most acts of love are not emotional but volitional (with deliberate intention). Simply, it is the best thing for my children. You demonstrate your love for them by acting out of obedience to the Word, your conscience, counseling you've received, or some moral compass. And the child's response of obedience shows his or her love for you. There are no emotions (well hopefully), just obedience.

Sacrificial, unreciprocated acts and expressions are love at its deepest level. God used an ancient Greek word when He called this *agape* love. When Jesus challenged Peter three times about whether he loved Him, as recorded in John 21, the third time was, "Do you *agape* Me?" And the sacrifice of His Son for us was the ultimate act of *agape* love.

There is a moving video on YouTube that I have watched several times.[18] Maybe you have seen it too. The true story is one of the most selfless acts of love at the deepest level I have ever witnessed. I won't do it justice, so I encourage—no, demand—that you do a Google search for *ironman triathlon, Dick and Rick Hoyt* and view it for the full impact. But I'll do my best to demonstrate the *agape* love between a father and his son. The young man and his dad race in many Ironman events throughout the world as a team. Why together? Because the son is a paraplegic. They (or should I say, the dad) race, bike, and swim. The father has dedicated himself to joyously allow his son to fulfill his passion. Because of the sacrifices that the father has had to make in training and enduring strenuous physical and mental demands, he wins my father of the decade vote. He simply does it because he loves his son. Are any of us willing to make that effort, putting aside our selfish pleasures for the good of our children? Maybe there are some other equal heroes. We need more.

Emotional love is good and volitional love is good, but together, they are great. Hugging, kissing, high fiving, pats on the back or butt, encouraging words, and verbal expressions of "I love you" all show your love for your child. But there are times when emotions must be set aside and hard volitional decisions must be made. Some might call some of these decisions "tough love." These are no less love—necessary, yes, but no less love.

It has been said that love covers a multitude of sins. As fathers, we make every mistake in the book; at least I did. But if your children know you love them, even the poor decisions are accepted by them, especially if they are accompanied by a plea for forgiveness. For those of you who have just started this re-engagement process, you may have a lot for which you need to seek forgiveness. This might take some time, especially for them to forgive. And for their health, they eventually need to forgive you. Don't dump all of the issues on them at one time. Start showing them how much you love them and work in all the items that need addressing during the occasions that offer the best opportunity.

The Bible, in 1 Corinthians 13, tells us that there are three things we live on—faith, hope, and love, and the greatest of these is love. Nothing can equal or replace it in a relationship. Being honest and truthful is a good place to start in expressing your love. I guarantee in later years your children will look back and say that their father made a lot of mistakes, but they always knew he loved them. What confidence that instills in children and eventual adults. When they understand they are loved by their father, then they are prepared to live lives that are filled with faith and hope. Without that assurance, it is virtually impossible to develop a life with these attributes.

There is a game called Show and Tell. Love operates the same way. How can I show my children how much I love them, and when will be the next occasion to tell them? And we are not talking about buying them off with money or things. Show and tell love involves you with them. There is no greater gift than yourself, with all your warts and shortcomings. God gave His greatest gift to us: Himself, through His Son. And He did not make a mistake when He made you their father. The greatest commandment in the Scriptures, both Old and New Testaments, is, "Love the Lord your God with all your heart and with all your soul and with all your mind. And the second is like it—love your neighbor as yourself" (Matt. 22:37–40 NIV). How could you have a closer neighbor than your own flesh and blood? Look no further than your own children. You just may get a blessing in return. They could just start loving you back. Wouldn't that be special?

I have saved this for last, purposefully. The subject matter embraces a whole other book. Make no mistake, fathers, if you do not love your children's mother and demonstrate it, the majority of your teaching and instruction will most always fall on deaf ears. Why? Because you will come across eventually as a hypocrite and your kids can spot it a mile away. They have a nose for it. Your words and actions to them become empty, void of any substance. This is where modeling really takes shape. Way too many households are held together "for the sake of the kids." But really, you might as well light a stick of dynamite under them with a long fuse. Eventually, it will explode, and it will be a mess. Do not try to fool them. If you are having trouble in your marriage as it relates to their mother, then bare your soul and seek forgiveness and restitution. Deal with it. The Scriptures are very clear on this. Ephesians 5:25 NKJV exhorts us, "Husbands, love your wives, just as Christ also loved the church and gave Himself up for her." Easy, no; possible, yes. Alone, no; with God's help, yes. Worthwhile, you bet. Necessary, absolutely! This may be the very first place your journey must start.

Questions to Ponder:

Did you hear your father say he loved you, and how does that make you feel?

Have you ever said, "I love you" to all your children?

Are you willing to start the process by doing this?

Would you children say that you love them, and also, do you *unconditionally* love them?

List some specific ways you will adopt to show your love. (Use extra paper if required.)

CHAPTER 5: A'PRAYING

Devote yourselves to prayer, keeping alert in
it with an attitude of thanksgiving.

—*Apostle Paul*
Colossians 4:2 NASB

If I were to share an absolute that overrides any other attribute in a father, it is being prayerful. Many men will tell you this is just not necessary. I must admit, I have known apparently successful fathers with good children who probably have never uttered a prayer. But I submit that you as a father have to determine what you want to ultimately accomplish in your parenting as an end result in your children. As for me, I must admit that I alone was not wise or strong enough to pull it off, so I sought divine guidance through prayer.

Some of you will jump all over this, while many are right now saying, "Bill, I have never prayed in my life, and I've turned out okay." Still others respond that they don't even know what prayer is or how one goes about praying. And I bet you skeptics are thinking, *That's okay for little old women but not for me.* Many have experienced or heard stories about asking God for something and it never happening. "I prayed that my daddy would get well when I was a child, and God let him die anyway." No doubt there are a myriad reactions to the thought of praying in general, and especially for one's children.

Prayer is a complex subject but really quite simple too. It is okay to say, "I don't know how to pray." The first disciples of Christ confessed that to Jesus when they were with Him. He did not condemn them but taught them the Lord's Prayer as recorded in Matthew 6:9–13. He gave them a format for prayer. He then left it up to them to fill in the blanks based on their hearts' desires and needs.

Many believe the only prayer God hears from an unrepentant sinner is one in which the person seeks forgiveness for their sins, confessing they cannot save themselves and trusting Jesus Christ for their salvation. With that, His Holy Spirit takes up residence in their lives and then starts teaching them how to pray and what to pray for.

Some of you may want to pause and do business with God right now. At the very back of this book, I have printed out a prayer you might want to use if it expresses the desire of your heart. Know that the prayer is not what saves you but your act of faith when you trust Christ secured by His death on the cross. He then rose from the dead and offers life in Him for eternity.

The Bible has extensive writings on prayer. You may want to dust off yours or get a new one that has a concordance that will direct you to chapter and verse. And for you high-tech guys, the Internet is stocked with ways and means to surf the Bible on any subject; so each of us is without excuse. Access is there. Make the effort!

Simply, prayer is sharing with God what is on your heart and listening to Him by whatever means He chooses to speak. After one has developed a personal relationship with God through His Son, Jesus, a reservoir of treasures is available through prayer. Even miracles might happen, like your children turning out well in spite of your fathering or lack thereof. If you believe that, and I do, God gave these specific children to you to raise for Him, and He knows their needs far greater than you ever will, why then does it not make sense to call on Him for His help? As an example only, if you have a bank account with millions of dollars in it at your disposal and family is starving each month and struggling to survive, would it not make all the sense in the world to draw on that account to enhance their lives, if not save them? There are so many promises in the Bible, and He pleads with us to ask, seek, and knock. It implies that He will hear and is willing and able to assist. And unlike us earthly fathers, He knows what is actually best for you as a father and your children.

Being a father is probably the world's greatest, and hardest, task anyone undertakes. Many of you are nodding approval to this. Men, it simply is a giant responsibility. Some of you command strategic positions in business or other places. Would you dare undertake the objectives of your position without securing the best possible help and advice you could afford to ensure success? Well, for the job of father, you have the best possible help, and it is absolutely free and inexhaustible. It is called *prayer*.

For some of you, prayer should start with confession that you cannot or have not done the job well or that might be required. Do you know to confess really means to agree with God? He already knows you are inadequate. You are not surprising Him. Just admit it, repent of it, and seek His help. You will be amazed by the many ways He starts sending help.

For others, it is simply fine tuning your prayer life and re-attuning your ears to His voice.

And the very best way to hear that voice is through reading and listening to Him through His word, the Bible. It makes your prayer life more effective.

If you will permit me, I would like to give a word of testimony about my prayer life as it relates to my family, children, and now grandchildren. I have always had some form of prayer life since I was a kid. But several years ago, it was impressed on me that I, in my limit of time and space, could not be with, care for, and direct every moment of my children's lives. As my prayer life started developing, it became abundantly clear that my most effective parenting tool was, in fact, prayer. Since God is omnipresent, and I am not, why should I not turn them over to Him each day, by faith through prayer on their behalf, today and for eternity?

So, that is just what I do. Briefly speaking, I submit them every morning to His care, and I pray for them by name for many different issues and needs. And during the day, as I am reminded, I submit prayers on their behalf. I find strength, comfort, and peace from trusting them to the One who made them, as He knows far greater than I the needs in their life, moment by moment. And since He is also omnipotent (all-powerful) and omniscient (all-knowing), what could be better than Him for the welfare of my children and grandchildren?

My life verses are Matthew 6:33–34 NKJV: "But seek first the kingdom of God and His righteousness, and all these things (all we need) shall be added to you. Therefore, do not worry about tomorrow, for tomorrow will worry about its own things. Sufficient for the day is its own trouble." Every day is a gift. It has its own set of problems. To me, life is a box of envelopes filled with the provisions for that day. Yesterday's provisions are all used up, and tomorrow is not yet here. By living one day at a time, I can start that day by opening the new envelope and know that today's needs are sufficiently provided for. And it reminds me that I need to be in prayer early on and trust God with the day—for my wife, my children, and my grandchildren. Certainly, there are other items involved in prayer, but as it relates to me as a father, I have that privilege and responsibility as a father for my own. This requires that you seek out, inquire, and observe the needs of the family so you may pray more effectively. God will lead you in the way to pray for them.

One of our pastors recently delivered a sermon on a Puritan creed of sorts: "Pray until you pray." What? All of us at times pray idle or insincere prayers, some without much thought.

They are sort of rote or routine. What the Puritans were saying was to become involved in what and how you are addressing the Lord on whatever subject. Stay there long enough until you start sensing a spiritual depth in your praying, a oneness with God, as if you could reach out and touch Him. James 4:8 NKJV tells us, "Draw near to God, and He will draw near to you." And further, Paul writes "be anxious for nothing, but in everything by prayer and supplication with thanksgiving let your requests be known to God. And the peace of God, which surpasses all comprehension, will guard your hearts and your minds in Christ Jesus" (Phil. 4:6–7 NASB) Want that kind of peace?

If I did not firmly believe that there are forces at work daily to take my children down, then I would have no need for prayer. But since I do believe this, I pray as if it all depends on me but trusting God with the results. Call me old fashioned and out of step, but it simply is what allows me to function each day, knowing they are safely in His hands. It doesn't mean bad things won't happen, but I have the assurance that it is being filtered through His loving hands.

Recently, I heard one of my daughters say to someone that one of the things she remembers as a child was seeing her father praying for her and what that meant to her. And I have heard testimony after testimony from others about this very same subject. Can you even imagine the confidence children must sense when they see or know their father is praying on their behalf? At different times, I have journaled my prayers. Joanne does this daily, as do countless others. You get to see God's hands at work, and recording it builds faith to continue and to be bold in your requests.

But equally, if not more important, is the habit of praying with your children. For younger kids, the nighttime tuck-in by Dad and prayer with each one cannot be measured. First, you become the teacher on how to pray, and second, you become the conduit for them to the Heavenly Father. They see God through you.

For older ones, specific times of prayer are well received. They can be about questions, issues, or trials; you name it. There is simply something good that happens to both of you when you pray with a child. You can have prayers at meals, at home or when dining out or over the phone when away or during the day when they call and are in need of your counsel. You can bet that they will call a dad they know will pray for/ with them. All are sending the message that you think prayer is important.

And I strongly recommend you not develop the habit of saying, "I'll pray for you about this or that," because most of us won't. Pray right then and later if you are reminded. Let's face it, guys, you do not know everything about everything. And most importantly, after three years of age, your children know it. So why call on a limited reserve of knowledge? Instead, tap into a full tank of wisdom. God tells us in James 1:5, "If we lack wisdom, ask Him, and He will give it to you liberally and without reproach" (my translation).

For you macho, thump 'em on the head' guys, this part of fatherhood may be difficult at best. I know a big guy. When I first met him in the '70s, he was, to me, the biggest guy I had ever met. He starred as a lineman in the NFL when men were men and was a four-time All-Pro for the Cleveland Browns. He spends a lot of time in prisons, talking and preaching to men. He wrote a book that I recommend highly and give away to many fathers of every age. His name is Bill Glass, and the book is *Champions for Life.* I bet you can relate to him. And he prays. Imagine that.

No prayer is too small or insignificant in the eyes of God. Scripture tells us that Jesus is our High Priest and is interceding for us 24/7 at the right hand of His Father. That says to me that He just might be interested and available to handle your requests. He gave you this family and made you their "priest," and the "shepherd" of your flock. Call on Him. He is waiting—no, eagerly waiting—to hear from you. His number is toll free. Dial Him up. You'll enjoy the conversation. For those who have not called in a while, take time to catch up with Him before making your requests. He will appreciate that.

Questions to Ponder

Are you a man of prayer? Do you believe God cares?

How often do you pray? Is that adequate?

Do you pray specifically for each of your children?

Do they know you pray for them?

Do you pray with them?

Have you ever tried praying and then truly waiting on God to act?

CHAPTER 6: A'MODELING

People may doubt what you say, but they will believe what you do.[19]

— Lewis *Cass*

"Better caught than taught" is an age old adage, and it is true. In most instances, *actions do speak louder than words.* Children, at most every age, but certainly from one to six, absorb everything and process it as truth. After that, it seems their minds start challenging what they have learned. They have an enormous capacity. Try to understand that they know nothing upon entering this world, so all is new to them. And because of a keen interest, they focus on each new bit of data, and it becomes uniquely stored, both consciously and subconsciously. Believe this grandfather, they watch your every move. In fact, they will start anticipating your actions after a while. For the most part, everything they have learned up to this point has shaped their lives.

So what are you modeling that you want your children to catch, especially the eldest child? Eldest children have no older siblings to learn from; so, Dad, for the most part, you're it. I earlier mentioned a 1974 folk rock song with a wealth of profound truth, "Cat's in the Cradle" by Harry Chapin. The words are chilling if you are a father. It is reprinted in its entirety in chapter one. But one of the most telling lines is by the son: "He'd say, I'm gonna be like you, dad. You know I'm gonna be like you." And toward the end the woeful father exclaims,

"He'd grown up just like me. My boy was just like me." Do you want your children to be "just like you"? For some of you, it might be affirmative, but for many, it is frightening.

As you are modeling, you need to make sure your children understand you are not the perfect model. Your children need to see your scars and know that you have made mistakes. They should hear through you that there are consequences to detouring and following wrong paths. Transparency is a strength. They need to see your weaknesses, because many children place their father on a pedestal, with the image that dear ol' dad has always had it all under control. This transparency will endear them to you and give them the assurance that it is okay to fail, knowing you did in certain ways, but you got back in the game of life and moved on.

Since a model is supposed to represent or reflect that which the *designer/creator* intended:

What are you trying to reflect?
What/who is the *original* you are trying to represent?
What do you want your children to see in you?

Would you be willing to say what Paul said to Timothy as recorded in 1 Corinthians 4:16 NKJV: "Therefore I urge you, imitate me"? Later he exhorts his followers: "Be imitators of me (*how?*), just as I also am of Christ." Jesus was the *model of humility,* and how did this play out? He said clearly in John 5:19 NKJV: "Most assuredly, I say to you, the Son can do nothing of Himself, but *what He sees the Father do*; for whatever He does, *the Son also does in like manner.*" He also said, "He who has seen Me has seen the Father …" (John 14:9b NKJV) Here it is again—a "spitting image." He simply modeled His Father's attributes, and they are endless.

When I was a child, model airplanes were big for us kids, especially boys. We had all the necessary parts, and we had the plans, so we proceeded to follow instructions and create our model plane. How well we followed the instructions and attended to each detail determined the end result, whether it was a shabby one or a pristine copy. The model was to resemble the real plane. It was simply a model, a representation on a smaller scale. Isn't that what our children are becoming, a representation of you on a smaller scale?

We have all said or heard, "Your kid is a chip off the old block," or "Your child looks and acts just like you." Scary? I hope not, but maybe. Apples don't fall far from the trees. So what fruit is your modeling going to produce? Fruit trees take a long time to grow from seedlings before they produce their fruit. Your children are no different. They have a limited number of years before they start reproducing what they have seen and heard and been taught. Apple trees simply do not produce peaches. The seeds of reproduction are in the fruit. If you have planted and nurtured your "fruit trees," they will bear the intended fruit and they, in turn, will most likely plant these same seeds in the next generation.

But have you ever visited an orchard of any kind that was not cared for, overgrown, overrun with pests, un-pruned, and un-fertilized or watered? It's not a pretty sight, and the worst part is the sad nature of the fruit, if there is any. A man who would develop a fine orchard would be considered a fool to let it go unattended. Why plant the trees if you are not going to care for them? So it is with your offspring, your seedlings. They need nurturing, pruning (disciplining), and loving care. What do you want your future "orchard" to look like? What does it require from you to accomplish that?

One of the most graphic illustrations is male and female models on TV, in magazines, in stores, or on runways at showings. Our society is bombarded with them. Our culture is consumed by them. What Madison Avenue is selling is a look that is right for you. Every model has gone through strenuous regimens to present the "perfect image." *"I'd die to look like them"* many of us say. What we are seeing is ourselves looking that way in that outfit or whatever the model is displaying.

Most of humanity could never look like them. We're short, fat, not so handsome, and so on. But we can at least imagine, can't we? That is the purpose of modeling—to create a desire in another to be like them. All of you remember the Marlboro Man. He made people think, *If I smoke Marlboros, I will be ruggedly handsome, free spirited, and much more.* I must confess, during my few short years of smoking, all I ever really got was a bad taste and cough.

Model in *Webster's*, when used as an adjective, means, among other things, "worthy of imitation," as in model citizen. And as a noun, it means "someone worthy of imitation," as in "every child needs a role model."[20] Are you attempting to be that for your kids? *You should not expect to be perfect but pursue the high calling.*

Take a look at the model you are presenting.

Honestly evaluate the areas that you believe, if copied, would be harmful and/or detrimental to the next generation, your children.

Set goals to improve in these areas. Focus on the positive modeling you are doing and further refine these.

Ask your kids and your spouse what they see that is good or bad. They know you best.

As in the song, you just might be blessed to hear your child proudly say one day, "I turned out just like you dad, I turned out just like you." Is that not worth all the effort you can bring to your parenting?

Questions to Ponder

Are you modeling what you want your children to emulate?

What actions are you modeling that need correcting?

Would your children consider you one of their chief role models?

Do you want them to turn out just like you?

CHAPTER 7: A' MENTORING

Never tell me the sky's the limit when
there are footprints on the moon.

—Unknown

Mentoring is seen in every walk of life. It really is different from modeling. Effective mentoring is intentional—pro-active, not reactive. Mentors are teachers, counselors, advisors, and yes, to a certain extent, role models, but not necessarily. Being a mentor involves a certain level of trust. Please know that many of you have tried, and may still be trying, to become your child's best friend. Make certain to hear this. In rare instances, this may occur, but it is not a primary objective. If that is your goal, then failure in many areas of your parenting will occur because you will compromise certain key areas just to be liked by the child. How can you be a best friend when you have to discipline, or make hard decisions that are best for them? If that eventually happens, *touchdown!* But don't make it a priority.

Webster's defines mentor as "a wise and trusted guide and advisor."[21] You are dealing with wisdom in this area of fatherhood. Recognize that you cannot possibly know everything that will be asked of you by your children. Much of what they are growing up in was not even around when you were developing as a man. So how can you be an "all-wise sage"? Simply, it involves *wisdom*. And since it appears none of us are born with much, how is it attained and disbursed?

1) Sitting under, observing, and learning from wise people in all walks of life.

2) Meditating on the wisdom books of the Bible—Proverbs and Ecclesiastes as starters.

3) Hanging out with strong father figures.

4) Reading and studying prominent men of faith.

5) Examining your own strengths and weaknesses in this area.

6) Seeking assistance in areas in which you have no experience.

7) Practicing the art of saying, "I don't know, but I will get back to you."

8) Praying to God, the true source, for adequate wisdom to be an effective father/husband.

Did schools hand out prophylactics when you were in school? If yes, you are a very young father. When you were young, were laptop computers and iPhones even invented with instant access to everything online? Let's face it—your kids are more exposed to things you know very little about. My oldest grandson is fourteen, and since he was about ten, he has all but mastered the computer world. Every answer to virtually every question he might want to know is accessible to him and his peers today in sometimes less than a minute on their handheld.

Ask them who won the World Series fifty years before they were born. In a moment, they can pull up that data and have more information than you could ever remember or hope to know, so don't try to be all-knowing. You will fail the test, and they will stop coming to you for the important issues of life, like:

Does God exist?
Why did my best friend shoot himself?
Should I join the Scouts?
Which sport should I spend time on?

Why do the boys just not like me?
What school is best for me?
Is Jesus God?
What should I do when my best friend turns on me?
Do you think I'm pretty?
Do you really understand how hard it is to grow up today?
Why is it wrong to have sex outside of marriage?
Do you think Jesus is the only way to be saved?
What do you believe about evolution and creation?
Where do babies go when they die at birth?

There are a million of these. And if asked, they are important to the child. These are moral, ethical, spiritual, and social issues that affect them. They need answers or at least a dialogue. It is never wrong to say, "I don't know." Most of their questions are not math or English. They are things that mold and shape the society in which they are growing up. Many are gray areas, without concrete answers. That is okay. Saying, "I'll get back to you on that" is all right too or "Let's set a time to get back about that question." You will be showing wisdom. But definitely get back to them soon. They are waiting.

Much of the time, they just want to communicate with you, and by keeping the door open, you are encouraging them to do so. After a tough date, or a severe disappointment, you want them to feel free to come to you about anything. You have to earn this right. Some kids say, "I can't talk to my dad about anything; he will just give me a lecture." You do not want them to go elsewhere for comforting or answers. And you really don't want them to bottle things up inside of them. That is very dangerous. I know I did that way too often to my girls. That is what is so good about being a grandfather; you can just listen. Most of the time, that is all they wanted anyway.

In James 1:5–7 NASB, the writer exhorts us, "But if any of you lacks wisdom, let him ask of God, who gives to all men generously and without reproach, and it will be given to him.

But let him ask in faith without any doubting, for the one who doubts is like the surf of the sea driven and tossed by the wind. For let not that man expect that he will receive anything from the Lord, being a double-minded man, unstable in all his ways." We discussed this earlier. You have been given the responsibility to be your children's mentor, something like a counselor. You have to be prepared, ready at a moment's notice. And it is imperative that you have a resource(s) to employ for the most truthful and helpful answer or advice. They want and deserve answers; you need wisdom. They do not want made-up answers—homespun wisdom with no real solution or depth.

That is why, to me, there is no greater source of wisdom than the Holy Scriptures. I believe they were inspired by God, delivered to us by His Holy Spirit through those like you and me who were facing the same situations. I firmly believe truth is certain and not relative. Shades of truth do not exist, and your kids need solid shaping truth. The book of Proverbs was written with you in mind. But you have to read, study, and meditate on them. There is one or more for most every situation—and possibly every question. But you have to be equipped. What does God say to us in His word about this? These are only selected verses out of many:

> Proverbs 2:6 NASB , "For the Lord gives wisdom; from *His* mouth come knowledge and understanding. Look at Proverbs 2:1 NASB: "If you will receive my words … and treasure my commands within you …" Will you?

> Proverbs 3:1 NASB , "Do not forget my teaching, but let your heart keep my commandments."

> Proverbs 4:5 NIV, "Get wisdom, get understanding!"

> 2 Chronicles 1:10 NKJV , "Now give me wisdom and knowledge, that I may go out and come in before this people, for who can judge (*mentor*) this great people of Yours."

Ecclesiastes 7:12b NKJV, "Wisdom gives life to those who have it."

Micah 6:9b NASB, "It is sound wisdom to fear Your name."

Luke 2:52 NKJV, "And Jesus increased in wisdom and stature, and in favor with God and man."

Let's look at a couple of possible issues. This is a dialogue you might have with one of your children:

"Dad, is it okay to be wealthy?"

"Well, Proverbs tell us in 22:4 NKJV, and elsewhere, that "by humility and the fear of the Lord are riches, honor and life.""

"That"s awesome. Where did you learn that?"

"Oddly, as a businessman, I have also been dealing with that question, and recently in my studies I ran across this set of verses. I don"t have all the answers, so I"ve been tapping into greater resources than I."

"Wow, Dad! Do you see what that verse says? We can get more than just wealth; honor and life come along also. All we have to do, according to this verse, is to be a humble person and respect or fear the Lord. Sounds opposite to what I hear from a lot of other people. Thanks, Dad. That really has cleared up some issues in my life when I start making money."

And another one might be*:*

"Daddy, you have always stressed that we should always talk through things inside a family, and this is a very personal subject. These guys at school are always hitting on me and some of my friends to have sex with them. Some of my friends are into that, but you and Mom have always stressed that it is wrong. Is that just "old school" and now it"s all right? They say we are not really hurting anyone else and that it is an awesome feeling. So, how do I handle this? What should I do?"

"Well, sweetheart, I know the current times are different from mine in many ways at your age, but I have found truth is the same then as it is now. Times change but truth doesn"t. Sometime back I read 1 Corinthians 6 about sexual immorality being forbidden. "The body is not meant for sexual immorality, but for the Lord, and the Lord for the body." "And later it exhorted us to "flee from sexual sin." In Proverbs 4:23 NIV God tells us to "guard our heart for everything you do flows from it." Honey, when you engage in sex outside of marriage, you are opening your heart up to many things that will prove to be detrimental. I can sense that you believe it is wrong or else you would not be talking to your ol" Dad about such a sensitive subject. Guard your heart, my child; I know you will make the right decision."

"Daddy, you"re the greatest. Thanks."

Fathers, these are only two examples of issues with which you and your children will deal (or have already dealt). When you are mentoring, you are not always saying, "Don't do this, don't do that." You are offering wise counsel that they hopefully will embrace and make wise choices. You know it is best for them. They need to make that decision also. The wisdom they receive from you must be trusted. You can lead a horse to water, but you can't make him drink. You have given the best possible advice, you have trusted in the counsel, and more often than not, they will also. It will prove to be adequate most times.

Do not focus on your children but on the wisdom you are providing. Your children process this better when it is from a reliable source and they know you have their best interest in mind. And I have found, if it is bathed in prayer, it rarely fails to accomplish its objective.

Questions to Ponder

Are you the "go-to" mentor in your children's life?

Are they listening to and grasping your messages?

If not, what must you do differently?

What other resources do you need to employ in this role?

CHAPTER 8: A'LISTENING

I know that you believe you understand
what you think I said,
but I'm not sure you realize that what
you heard is not what I meant.[22]
—*Robert McCloskey*

Well, men, this is not our forte. At least it's not mine, or so I have been told throughout my life, mostly from those near and dear to me. But I must have listened at times or I wouldn't remember them telling me that I never listen. So, this is more of doing what I say rather than what I do.

Experts tell us that few men multi-task. If this is true, and I have experience that it is, then if I am reading or watching sports, how can I possibly hear a statement or question directed to me? Lay the book down, put the tube on mute, and listen. That is what we should do. But most of us just ignore it as if we did not hear, or at best, grunt as if we understood. Dangerous! And I have to admit that most wives cannot understand why we even have to do anything to hear them. "But honey, I want to hear what you have to say," He says. And the usual response by her is disgust that we actually had to stop what we were doing to hear them. Moving on!

Listening, I mean meaningful listening, is an art, a skill that can be mastered. For some, it is not, nor will it ever be easy. Most of us have to work hard at this. But if we are to hear and be respectful to others, it must be mastered. In today's noisy world of many sounds, it is especially difficult. And for us, the aging class, we don't have the keen ears we once had. Plus the many gadgets we have at our disposal that seem to hold our attention and distract us add stress to the listening process.

Maybe some of you men have problems with concentration or have selective listening that does not allow you to grasp the entire subject matter being directed toward you. I admit I have at times stopped listening for whatever reason. Either I got the gist of what was being said or was not interested in the rest of the story or discussion. Neither endears you to the other party. Have you ever noticed women talking to one another? They focus, look at each other, even if uninterested, and remember the conversation, every detail. We, on the other hand, listen like we are at a noisy cocktail party and would rather be somewhere else.

In James 1:19 NASB, we are exhorted to be "quick to hear, slow to speak and slow to anger." When Jesus would begin to teach the disciples a parable, He would tell them to listen to this or say, "Verily, verily," or "hear My words." He knew they and we are prone to drift off and lose the impact of the message. "Hear, O Israel" resounds throughout the Old Testament when God or His prophets began to speak. This should comfort us to know we are not alone in this delinquency of listening. But it should also prompt us to understand the necessity of being a good listener.

This leads us to our children and their need for us to hear them. This is critical to continue keeping the communication open between you and them. Most times, all they want is to tell you something that requires no action on your part. For most men, therein lies the problem. We start thinking about how to solve the problem while they are still speaking to us. That is a good thing, as men are wired that way. But it is not in every situation, especially with your children or spouse. In the chapter on mentoring, we discussed a couple of hypothetical dialogues. In those cases, the child was asking for advice and counsel. But most times, children are expressing themselves only to be heard.

When you are an attuned listener, you hear the inflections, observe the body language, and more. All this helps determine the course of action or inaction. If we're focused on the solution during the conversation, we can miss so much more than the mere words. And lest we dare forget, being judgmental in our responses is the quickest way to sever all future dialogue with our children. Most times, if they are sharing heart issues or problems, just through the sharing, they arrive at the solution even without our input.

Developing good questions that you can ask will spark more dialogue. What you want to really happen, in most circumstances, is that they resolve it on their own without you saying a word. Good listeners cause that to happen. Here are some suggestions for me and you to follow. They are not all-inclusive by any measure but will be useful for constructive listening. This form of engagement says you really care about your children and what they have to say. In almost every situation, when someone asked Jesus a question, He answered them with one. Interesting, don't you agree?

Focus and concentrate.
Make eye contact when possible.
Listen for what might be unsaid.
Observe body language.
Ask pertinent questions as opposed to offering advice.
Comment on what you hear.
Repeat it to them when appropriate (did I hear that correctly?).
Use Scripture where necessary in offering solutions.
Learn to rejoice in what they are telling you.
Likewise, be empathetic when necessary.
Hugs sometimes are the best and maybe only answer after listening.

For youngsters, use meals or bedtime to ask them to speak of their day or issues.

Don't be afraid to say you don't know to certain questions. Pray with/for them if this appears appropriate.

Don't override them and disrupt their thoughts.

Never put them down when they share something with you.

Don't judge them if they have shared personal items.

Take older children out to a meal to open up conversational dialogue.

Ask them later about your discussions to show concern and interest.

If it is private about them or others, commit to not passing it on.

Do not be a party to gossip, even to the point of asking them to not share it.

Do not attempt to listen and text, and ask them to do the same.

Use family meals at home or dining out to be times of speaking and listening.

When your family has something to say to you, assume it is vital to them.

The art of quality listening has been lost on recent generations. For you, as a father, to be one that swims against the tide, it will reap great benefits for all concerned. It will teach your children that listening is vital to any relationship. I have often said that since God gave us two ears and only one mouth, He must want us to listen twice as much as we talk. I, for one, struggle with that ratio. Maybe writing this book will help me more than the other readers. I can only hope.

Recently, a man shared that his dying mother's doctor told him that even though she could no longer verbalize her thoughts, she could still hear him and that the ears are usually the last organ to fail. I observed that in my mother the last week of her life. That speaks volumes to me on the critical issue of listening. Scripture also tells us that faith that leads to salvation comes by hearing. Romans 10:17 NASB is clear on how vital it is to listen—really listen: "So faith comes from hearing, and hearing by the word of Christ."

Proverbs has numerous exhortations for young and old alike to listen. Following are a few: all of chapter 1; 4:1, 10, 20; 5:1, 7, 13; 7:24; 8:6, 32, 33; 13:1; 19:20; 22:17; 23:19, 22. Read them aloud and *listen* as if they were all written to you.

God speaks to us in many ways: through His creation, His word, and even our wife and children. *Are we listening?*

Questions to Ponder

How would you rate your listening skills?

Do you take time to hear your children and your wife?

How would they describe you in this area?

What steps are necessary to improve your listening?

CHAPTER 9: A'TEACHING

*Give a man a fish, and you feed him for a day; teach
a man to fish and you feed him for a lifetime.*

—Chinese Proverb.

Teaching is not to be confused with mentoring or modeling. A mentor or role model does not fulfill many of the requirements in life, from basic things all the way to exotic. Proverbs 4:1,2 NASB is the foundation for teaching: "Hear, O sons, the instruction of a father, and give attention that you may attain understanding. For I give you sound teaching; do not abandon my instruction." Law is "doctrine" or "teaching." The writer uses the word "instruction" of a father. In Deuteronomy 6:6–9 NKJV, God tells His people, as it relates to His commandments, to "teach them *diligently* to your children … when you sit in your house … walk by the way … lie down and … rise up." That doesn't leave much room, does it? You and I are to be diligent teachers, first of God's word and much, much more.

Teaching your children the truth in Scripture will ensure they will carry this all the days of their lives. God says, "My word will not return void." What He is saying to us is it will accomplish its purpose. What are some of the other things we should be teaching (instructing) our children? Here is but a sampling:

How to tie shoelaces

How to dress appropriately

Eating and social manners

Respect

Honesty

How to handle, shoot, and clean a gun safely

How to tie a square knot

How to hold a pencil

How to read and write

How to write and address a letter

How to write a check

How to use a computer

How to tell time

God's word

How to plant a seed

How to cook

How to make homemade ice cream

How to listen

How to pronounce words

How to ride a bike

How to paddle a canoe

How to ski

How to feed and care for pets

How to mow the yard

How to fly a kite

Right from wrong

How to hold a racket

How to drive

Integrity

Fundamentals of golf

How to play games or cards

How to sit

Health tips

How to shuck corn, snap green beans

How to clean a fish

How to sharpen a knife

Safety rules

How to swim

How to tie a fisherman's knot, bait a hook
How to brush teeth and hygiene
How to shave
Etiquette
How to skate and dance
How to throw and kick a ball
How to hit and catch
How to ride a wave
How to build sand castles
How to whistle
How to catch lightning bugs
How to pitch a tent
How to care for pets
Handling credit
Financial management
Business ethics
How to work

And while you are teaching countless things to them, you are demonstrating your love for them. You are saying, "You are important, and I want you to be well equipped for life and better able to handle it and enjoy it." And simultaneously, it also provides you the chance to let them see God's hand in all this. I recently started writing a series entitled *Life Speaks to Us* (www.lifespeakstous.com). A book by the same title has been published through CrossBooks. (Did you sense a commercial here?) The point of these writings is to draw attention to the myriad of lessons we can learn by observing God's creation. You have a chance to point these out and teach from them. Psalm 19 starts this way: "The heavens are telling of the glory of God, and the firmament is declaring the work of His hands. Day to day pours forth speech, and night to night reveals knowledge … Their line has gone out through the earth, and their utterances to the end of the world." We don't have to look far or read powerful books to have many opportunities to teach great and wonderful things to our children.

The list is endless. You and your children's mother will be involved in most of this. And as you teach the eldest, he or she, in turn, will be helping teach the younger ones. And I have found that this continues to future generations. Although it is more intense with pre-teens, there are a variety of things that only older children face. Be creative, and make it interesting. One of the joys as a grandfather is that you still get to do a lot of teaching. It never stops, and it never ceases being fun.

Fathers have to be present to teach. Absentee fathers miss out on a lot—and so do their children. Learning it the right way, from you, is simply special. I might add that you will be wise to delegate some of the teaching to others, certainly your wife, or someone well versed in the activity or circumstance. For instance, if your child is interested in golf or soccer, and you know nothing about either, wisdom would tell you to seek out someone who does.

I find the best opportunities to teach are those times not even designed for that specific purpose. Going camping with the family might create many related, or even unrelated, occasions to teach. A wise father will be constantly watchful for these opportunities. You are the chief empowerment for your child. And you need to be creative; make it interesting in a way that is easy to grasp and remember.

On our recent trip to the beach, all the older grandkids were riding boogie boards on the waves. Will, who has Down syndrome, kept watching all week, playing around the edges. Dad, Mom, and his three older siblings all took turns encouraging him, taking him farther and farther out. Then he started getting the hang of it. Fear seemed to give way to faith in them, the boogie board, and himself. During the last two days, he was on his own for the most part, riding the waves, getting up, plowing back out, and riding some more. Through this patient teaching, he was now empowered to handle this on his own. And I just bet he can't wait till next year to do it all week.

Interview any dedicated teacher and they will all tell you it is not for the pay that they do their jobs; it is the joy of teaching and empowering the next generation. While we certainly use trained teachers to educate our children, the best place to begin is with you teaching in the home. "Train up a child in the way he should go, and when he is old he will not depart from it" (Prov. 22:6 NKJV). And I might add he will pass it on to the next generation.

Questions to Ponder

What are you teaching your children?

Is it empowering them for their present and future endeavors?

What new things do they need to know with which you can assist them?

What forms of outside help do you need to fully train and equip them?

CHAPTER 10: A'DISCIPLINING

He who spares his rod hates his son, but he
who loves him disciplines him promptly.
—Proverbs 13:24 NKJV

Before addressing this section, I think it would be fair to say that if you are not addressing the previous roles as a father, it will be difficult to succeed in this area of discipline. Most likely you will be seen as a strict disciplinarian or "drill sergeant."

Here is a subject that stirs up debates, especially between old school and modern parents. But there is one thing about which most agree: children need to be disciplined in order to set parameters and boundaries, to learn good from bad, wrong from right, and respect. Fathers, this is your area of primary responsibility, like it or not. Whether it is the paddle or "time out," you are the innkeeper. Your wife gets her authority from and through you—but the buck stops with Dad.

It only takes a few months out of the crib until you find you are raising a *sinner*. Oh so cute but oh so selfish. "I want what I want and I want it now" is most children's attitude. Correcting this takes skill, patience, and training. "My daddy whipped my butt and I'm gonna whip yours" does not always work and neither does ignoring poor behavior. Left unaddressed, severe consequences most often develop, if not now, then later. I'm talking criminal in some instances.

Joanne and I grew up when Dr. Spock was touted to be the premier authority on child rearing. My parents were pre-Spock, if you get my drift. I might title it the "switch era" or paddle, maybe belt, even a razor strap. It can be very effective if used properly. My father never once disciplined me. Mother was assigned to the "switch patrol." Some people tell me that is why I was such a rotten kid. I might even agree. Later in my young life, she actually made me go choose the switch, and if it was less than adequate, she would choose the next one, bigger and stronger. The back of my legs felt the sting, but I never saw any anger. It appeared to fulfill her words, "This is gonna hurt me worse than it will you." My maternal grandfather, a big man at the time, who I respected and loved, was good at reaching for his belt or razor strap. He would fold it in both hands and snap it loudly two or three times. That worked for me. "I'm sorry" would come bellowing out of my mouth; even big ol' tears, too. And he never had to actually use it on my derriere, but I knew he would have if needed.

At my boy's prep school, the principal had a half-inch thick paddle with holes bored through the shaft with an appropriate handle. It was about two feet long. They never used it on me, but I knew it existed and the stories from other boys who had experienced the pain were enough for me. The procedure was bend over, grab your ankles, shut your eyes (praying as never before), and be prepared for one or more licks.

At certain ages, pain must accompany discipline. There has to be an association. Later, other methods are more appropriate. But wisdom would tell you that anger must not accompany the method. Firmness, yes. It is a part of teaching. The child must know the why. What you want the child to learn and the level of discipline must match the crime. Twenty lashes for a three-year-old saying, "I hate you" to his brother or a lecture and time out for five minutes after the six-year-old threatened his sister with a butcher knife are not appropriate for the action of the child. Certain destructive behavior needs to be nipped in the bud, and if they continue or worsen, either more appropriate and more severe punishment may be required, with possible professional help.

I might add, mothers should not make the father the bad guy, using the time-worn expression, "Just wait till your father gets home." This will undoubtedly cause damage to your image and your relationship with your kids; they will always fear your coming home. Most times, arriving home should be a joyous event, not an occasion for tumult. Some actions require immediate attention, and the one present must have the authority to execute the discipline. But there are certain occasions where the mother must delay until you arrive. Waiting can be harder for the child than the actual disciplinary action. It is the *fear of the unknown.*

One huge warning: the hand is never to be used as the instrument of choice for disciplining. The hand represents help, love, care, and comfort. To combine it with forms of whipping can be very confusing to the child, even breeding resentment. Confession—I have "dusted a few britches" with the only thing available, my open hand. Never have I felt good about the action after it was over. Never!

And while we are on hands, slapping or hitting of any nature are taboo—a no-no, never! Physical abuse usually starts here and then leads to worse forms of violent behavior. Experts will tell you, and the facts are there to confirm, children who experience any form of abuse most likely will become abusers themselves. One only has to read or listen to the news to know this is epidemic in America. It can be physical, verbal, or sexual abuse. None are acceptable. If you were abused in any way and sense your actions toward your family are developing in a similar manner, professional help should be sought immediately—hopefully at the very first sign. Fathers may take all their anger out on the spouse and never touch their children, but it is the same to them.

The Bible is very clear, with a number of Proverbs dealing with discipline. God must think it is worthy of our attention.

Proverbs 13:24 NKJV says, "He who spares his rod hates his son, but he who loves him disciplines him promptly."

Proverbs 19:18 NASB says, "Discipline your son while there is still hope, and do not desire his death."

Proverbs 22:15 NASB says, "Foolishness is bound up in the heart of a child; the rod of discipline will remove it far from him."

Proverbs 23:13,14 NASB says, "Do not hold back discipline from the child, although you beat him with the rod, he will not die."

Proverbs 29:15 NASB says, "The rod and reproof give wisdom, but a child who gets his own way brings shame to his mother."

Whatever your interpretation of the rod may be, it is not a tire tool or whip. You use a two-by-four on a donkey or mule to get his attention. That is fine for the beast of burden but not your precious children. But the rod must be firm enough to restrict and redirect the undesirable action of your child. It builds much-needed boundaries. They want it and need it. God instructs children to obey their parents. And to "honor your father and your mother, that your days may be prolonged in the land …" (Ex. 20:12 NASB). It is one of the original Ten Commandments with a promise. We have seen this next exhortation earlier, but it is worth repeating: "And, fathers, do not provoke your children to anger; but bring them up in the discipline and instruction of the Lord" (Eph. 6:4 NASB). Once the roots of bitterness take hold in the child toward the father, it may well take a lifetime to resolve the fallout, if ever. Much of the anger and bitterness develops from your means and methods of discipline. It is all supposed to show how much you love them, and it is designed to protect them and keep them from harm's way; to be blessed and be a blessing to others.

Most children know when they have erred and understand correction is needed. When you don't, they become confused. None want the consequences, but down deep they sense a need to be disciplined for their actions. And to not address the situation is sometimes worse. They wonder why now and not then. "What can I get away with?" becomes an overriding thought process for them. Scheming becomes second nature.

Some forms of disobedience need immediate correction, while others need to be delayed, but never for long. It may be you acknowledge the wrong but let the child know you may be too angry to make a wise decision. Or you may need discernment and time to discuss it with your wife or even seek counsel, if it is required. But *do* get back and *do* take some action. Children play the "divide and conquer" game with parents, and they do it well. When they do something that needs disciplinary action, they will try to drive a wedge between you and their mother. Then when you two start arguing or at least disagreeing, the child gently sneaks away and many times walks free. The answer is for you two to go elsewhere; discuss, debate, and decide. Then you re-engage the child with the appropriate punishment.

For older children, when you decide the method of discipline, be sure if it is over a set period of time, such as taking away their phone privileges for a week, that you follow through and monitor it. "Seven days is a week, son, not two." Sometimes we get to feeling guilty for the action we have taken. Renegotiating or release will always breed problems for the future. And if it is severe for an extended period, like all summer or a month, write out a contract identifying their action that caused your decision and the terms of the punishment. Have both of you sign with a stipulation that if it is not fully served as agreed, it may be extended for an indefinite period.

I have always heard that *a disciplined child is a happy child.* It is in your hands to accomplish this for your child—and to create a home where peace can exist. Without discipline in your home, unbridled terror will reign—and your child will become a cripple in many ways. You actually have between sixteen and eighteen years to assist your offspring in becoming a well-adjusted and productive adult.

Be consistent, firm, loving, and disciplining!

Questions to Ponder

Were you ever abused as a child in any way?

If so, are you dealing with it appropriately?

Describe yourself as it relates to disciplining. Be honest!

Have your methods been shown to be effective?

What areas do you need to change?

CHAPTER 11: A'BLESSING

*Hope sees the invisible, feels the intangible
and achieves the impossible.*

—Unknown

Fathers, as I was meditating on this quote from an unknown source, I thought about us. We are God's hope dispensers to our children. When we are pronouncing the blessing on our kids, that is what we become to them. We "lift their eyes" to horizons they would possibly never dream of on their own or without our encouragement. Do you see it—really see it? You help them *see* the invisible, *feel* that which is intangible, and *achieve* the impossible! I wonder what father sat at the edge of a bed night after night listening to his child plan to go to the moon one day, never discouraging the child or laughing at the improbable venture but dispensing hope that one day he or she could do just that. What a blessing!

This is something I never received; I mean a real, live blessing from my father. And while I attempted to do this to my daughters, I cannot point to a time and place. But I continued to attempt to *bless* them as best I knew how. Maybe there is some work still left for me. But one thing I do know now, it is vitally important. I alluded earlier to a book by Bill Glass entitled *Champions for Life*. I strongly recommend that every father and would-be dad read and study it. Once I consumed the material, I purchased numerous copies and

I still give it away to men. It is based on real-life experiences, both in his own life and from what he has experienced in his prison ministry for several decades.

Like Bill, I have spent over thirty years going to and teaching in prisons, juvenile detention centers, and homeless shelters. The stories seem to be the same. A father failed at his responsibility. Not only was the *blessing* not given, but there was also little, if any, guidance or love. It is as if they all went to the same school of absentee fathers. Few exceptions exist. Confused, lonely, angry—each man traveled the road of life, never sensing who he was, why he was here, and if anybody really cared about him.

So, what is a blessing? That's a good question that needs a clear answer. For me, it all appears to unfold with pagans as well as Jews and Christians. A blessing must be important, as one of the earliest Biblical recordings involves Jacob and his mother fraudulently obtaining Isaac's (the father's) blessing intended for Esau (see Gen. 27:1–29). Let's start with *Webster's* to get a generic understanding of the concept. "The act or words of one who blesses. Approval or encouragement." So, to *bless* is "to hallow or consecrate by religious rite or word"; "to invoke divine care for"; "to confer prosperity or happiness on"; "protect, preserve"; "endow, favor." Blessing is a noun, and bless is a transitive verb. In my mind it is *to transfer something that will be binding.* [23]

In the early Biblical cultures, the blessing was connected with inheritances, such as land and possessions. But it also included the name, the heritage, rite of passage, and much more. It is something you have not earned or deserved. It is an act of grace. And it was real and permanent. I find one of the most intriguing stories of blessing is Joseph, as described in Genesis. I challenge you to read and study his life in the context of his father's early blessing in Genesis 37–50. It is recorded that Jacob (now Israel) had twelve sons and that he loved Joseph more than all his sons. This set off a life of trouble for Joseph as his brothers, through jealousy, attempted to kill him; then they sold him to merchants as a slave. He ended up in the Pharaoh's service, was placed in authority, was thrown in jail for being falsely accused after resisting sexual advances by Potiphar's wife, found favor by interpreting dreams, and eventually restored all his family during a terrible seven-year famine with the blessing of Pharaoh. As one reads these chapters, it is overwhelmingly obvious that Joseph never lost sight of who he was. Even through his father's misguided handling of the family, the brothers' deceit, being exiled from his homeland, and suffering the wrath of a scorned suitor, he knew who he was and was secure in it. I submit it came from his father's early blessing.

When each child and grandchild was born, we dedicated them to God. But later I had to impress upon them the blessing that was theirs. They have been consecrated to the Lord. In other words, they were set apart to be used by Him and to be blessed by Him. As a father, you are the bearer of the blessing. They need to hear the words. They need to understand their destiny. What it says to them is monumental in terms of worth. As mentioned elsewhere, the Father *spoke* a blessing on Jesus, His Son, at His baptism. In Matthew 3:17 NASB, we read, 'and behold, a voice out of the heavens, said, "This is My beloved Son, in whom I am well-pleased."'

Look at this closely:

It was a voice—so it was spoken;

It was directed—this is;

It was personal—My;

It was affectionate—beloved Son;

It was between a father and the child—Son;

It was a distinct blessing—in whom I am well pleased.

You are okay; you are loved; you are accepted; you please me. This was directly pronounced on Jesus before witnesses. God was proud to say, "This is My Son, and I am pleased that He is."

Many fathers take their sons and daughters through a ceremonial rite of passage. This is what happened to Jesus. His life of ministry was about to enter its adult stage, so to speak. He heard the reassuring words from His Heavenly Father, "You have My blessing. Go and live, and die, victoriously." What confidence He must have had. No greater burden has any man in history ever had to bear. But He was prepared, because He had His Father's blessing.

One of the simple but yet profound thing a father's blessing bestows on a son or daughter is, "You are *complete*. You have what it takes. All that you are or will become is enough. You don't have to perform to earn the blessing. It has been bestowed on you. No one can diminish it. Life cannot squeeze it away from you. You are loved; you are significant; you are a winner."

How many kids, and adults, go through life thinking, wrongly, they are losers? Maybe, unfortunately, they heard those exact words from their father. How devastating. And they go through life fulfilling the prophecy. And with every failure, the hole in their heart gets deeper. One of the richest passages in Scripture that is the anecdote for this mindset is Psalm 139:14 NASB: "I will give thanks to You, for I am fearfully and wonderfully made; wonderful are Your works, and my soul knows it very well." My soul knows it very well. Fathers, did you hear that? Can you just sense the overflowing of confidence? To hear from your father that *you are awesome, complete, able, capable, and no mistake* is the strength for the road ahead. "Where's the door? Look out, world, here I come. Bring it on; I can handle it!" Well, that's what father's blessings do. Your words are shaping a person for life! What an ever-loving joy! son

Families in America, excluding certain ethnicities, have lost this. Maybe fathers just have not had the blessing and therefore they are unable to pass it on out of ignorance or pain from the lack of it. And even worse are the fathers who are not only not speaking a blessing but who are, in fact, expressing negative thoughts about their children. This lack of a spoken blessing and the wounds from hurtful words are producing a cripple, possibly for life. "Sticks and stones may break my bones, but words will never harm me." Since early childhood, kids have been shouting this to one another, as well as grown-up kids. Nothing could be further from the truth. Words kill! They kill self-esteem, goals, ambitions, dreams, hope, and much else.

But a well-thought-out blessing with an intended purpose gives life. And the son or daughter needs to hear it more than once. Memories, especially in the midst of trying circumstances, sometimes get clouded and the ability to recall your words spoken often into their lives may just be the medicine they need at that moment. As one example; maybe the temptation to do drugs arises, and it will. How your offspring think about themselves may be the deterrent. "No thanks, I don't need those. I am secure within myself. I am complete without them." Would you want to hear that testimony from your child? I would.

There are many wounds children encounter while growing up. There is one I would say is the most critical for a healthy child. And you, fathers, can go a long way to ensure that this does not happen to your children. It is the *father wound*. As a dad, you need to make sure they hear at least four things from you:

> *I love you.*
> *I'm proud of you.*
> *You're complete.*
> *You're good!*

And if you are the son, or daughter who has been wounded, there are reasons for you to even take the initial steps to reconcile the relationship. Not all fathers are good at communicating, and that may have been the problem all along. No one wants the un-bridged gap and the pain to continue.

For many, there have been several generations pass within your family tree who never received the blessing from their father. You can be the one who breaks this negative, generational heritage. Go and be blessed, and while you are going, stop long enough to pass along the blessing on your children. And for you who have older children, it is not too late. In fact, now just may be the best time for you to engage your offspring and pronounce a long-overdue blessing. "Pride goes before destruction, a haughty spirit before a fall," Proverbs 16:18 in the NIV tells us. Do not let pride stand in your way. Do it before it is too late.

And before we leave this subject, I want to introduce you to a very recent new friend. Greg Vaughn was moved by God's hand several years ago to address fathers and their impact of a written legacy to the next generations. His book and ministry, *Letters from Dad*, have become a best seller and a national outreach to countless thousands of men. This is powerful testimony to what a written word from a father's heart can do for a child. These can be treasures for now and generations to follow.

Including Bill and Greg, there are many qualified men living today who have published books and articles dealing with a father's blessing. There are organizations dedicated to the role of fathers. DVDs, websites, and seminars are available. Men, we are without excuse. And don't forget God's word. It is the book of blessings!

Questions to Ponder

Did you ever receive a blessing from your father?

Would it have made a difference in your life? If so, how?

Have you ever given a blessing to your children?

If so, how have they responded?

If not, what is your plan to do so?

THE CHALLENGE

•OVER THE NEXT <u>TWENTY-FOUR HOURS</u>

–GET <u>ALONE</u> AND SPEND <u>ONE HOUR</u> IN PRAYER

–PRAISE AND WORSHIP FOR MAKING YOU A FATHER

–FOR HIS GUIDANCE AND PRESENCE IN YOUR LIFE

–DEDICATE EACH CHILD TO HIM BY NAME

–FORGIVENESS FOR THE FAILURES AS A FATHER

–ABILITY TO BE AN ABIDING FATHER IN ALL AREAS

–AND WHATEVER IS ON YOUR HEART AS A FATHER AND HUSBAND

FOLLOWED BY

•DURING THE NEXT <u>SEVEN DAYS</u>

–WRITE EACH CHILD A <u>HAND WRITTEN</u> LETTER

–TELL EACH YOU LOVE THEM AND HOW IMPORTANT THEY ARE TO YOU

–THAT YOU HAVE COMMITTED TO PRAY FOR THEM BY NAME EACH DAY

–THAT YOU ARE THERE FOR THEM NO MATTER WHAT

ONE LAST THING!

•OVER THE NEXT <u>TWELVE MONTHS</u>

–PRAY, PLAN AND PERFORM A SPECIAL CEREMONY OF BLESSING FOR EACH CHILD OVER TEN. VIDEO AND

PRESENT IT TO THEM IN A SPECIAL TREASURE CHEST FOR THEM TO KEEP AND PASS ON TO THEIR CHILDREN.

–EACH CHILD IS UNIQUE SO BE ORIGINAL.

–AT ANY NEW BIRTH, PLACE YOUR HANDS ON THEIR HEAD AND IN THE PRESENCE OF FAMILY AND WITNESSES, DEDICATE THEM TO GOD! YOU ARE HIS PRIEST AND ELDER IN YOUR FAMILY.

CHAPTER 12: A'PROVIDING AND A'PROTECTING

But if anyone does not provide for his own, and especially for those of his household, he has denied the faith and is worse than an unbeliever.

—1 Timothy 5:8 NASB

We won't spend much time on these, but that does not mean they are any less important. They have been combined for a reason, not that they both start with a p. Simply, they are primarily what men or fathers do for their family. Men have been in this role for centuries. We were designed for this by our Creator. The cave man knew this from early on. We are the "hunters," and women are the "nesters." "Real men" provide and protect.

When we think of provide, it brings to mind food, clothing, and shelter. Certainly, many wives contribute to this, and they do it well. In certain families, the children are involved or have to be due to difficult financial circumstances. It should not be viewed as a chauvinist position but merely God's plan for the family. The father has been designated as head, so the plan and execution primarily fall in his area of responsibility, even if he is not the primary bread winner.

Providing for the family extends well beyond these three "biggies" for the father. There are many emotional and psychological issues that he is suited to handle and should embrace on behalf of the family. But as we all know, women are so gifted in these areas that to overlook their input and contribution would be a travesty. Much of the facets of providing is incorporated in the other chapters in this book.

And it is not buying off your kids. While you are about being the provision agent in your home, you should be empowering them so that they can be productive agents eventually in their homes. Bring them into your world. Let them see what this part of your arena looks and feels like. It will build a sound structure for their future.

I find that some fathers use their provision responsibility as something that they wrongly utilize for leverage in their family. They are so consumed with their self-importance that they invariably alienate their kids and wife. They have a "I make the money so I make the rules" kind of attitude. There is a golden rule saying, "He who has the gold makes the rules." But when fathers, men, rightly know their role and do not abuse it, they can prosper the family in many ways. "God resists the proud, but gives grace to the humble" (Prov. 3:34 NKJV). To be the best provider, a father needs to humbly recognize that the true provider is God Himself and by grace we are only the conduits. Kids will learn great lessons for their lives from this attitude. "Pride goes before destruction, and a haughty spirit before a fall" (Prov. 16:18 NKJV). How many times have we seen others, or even ourselves, so enamored with our assets and position and then to have the world come tumbling down around them/us? "For riches certainly make themselves wings; they fly away like an eagle toward heaven" (Prov. 23:5 NKJV). We need to stay anchored in Him and His provisions. He will never fail us.

Elsewhere, I have mentioned that Matthew 6:33–34 are my life verses in the Bible. In the previous verses dealing with wealth leading up to these two, Jesus is comparing us to birds, lilies, and grass. He is telling His listeners and us to not worry or be anxious about food, clothing, and shelter; rather, we are more important to Him than these and instead of pursuing the perishable, we should be seeking the imperishable. These are His kingdom and His righteousness! And His promise is clear; all these things will be added unto us. See, there is so much more in providing than just being a diligent worker, trying to accumulate. Children are watching their earthly provider, which hopefully will give them a clearer picture of their Heavenly Provider.

> *For wisdom is protection just as money is protection,. but the advantage of knowledge is that wisdom preserves the lives of its possessors.*
> *—Ecclesiastes 7:12 NASB*

Now on to protector. All you macho types have been waiting for this. "Yeah, now this is what I'm talking about! Don't nobody mess with my kids if'n they know what is good for them." Well, that's not quite what we are addressing. But close. "Blood is thicker than water" is for the most part a truism. Yes, there should be an attitude that I am here to protect my wife and kids from any and all things. Men are essentially designed to be that in their families. And no one respects a man who won't. Oh, did I say respect? It starts in the school yards and carries on for most of men's lives. Defending your honor, or your girl's, or kids', or family's is paramount. I'd have to say it is inbred. Respect is so basic to a man's self-esteem. Even Paul in Ephesians 5:33 NKJV points out this need as it relates to the most intimate of relationships, marriage. "Nevertheless let each one of you in particular so love his own wife as himself; and let the wife see that she respects her husband."

Watch other men or yourself in certain dangerous situations. Primarily, who do your kids turn to? Our senior pastor told a humorous story about this when his kids were younger. Some boy threw a ball on purpose at one of his girls and hit her in the head and hurt her. Immediately, he found the nearest ball and proceeded to nail the other kid in the forehead. That'll teach him to harm my kid. It was a wrong reaction to a bad situation, he admitted, but we are simply wired that way. Slow to anger might be the better remedy, as is taught in the Scriptures. But look at Jesus using His righteous anger when in Jerusalem; He encountered the abuse of His Father's house of worship. He turned over the tables of the money changers and scolded them for their actions. They were messing with His Father's house!

Recently, my eldest daughter walked into her daughter's sixth grade classroom to distribute Christmas gifts to the teachers. Without warning, a boy punched out another one and started screaming obscenities. With blood splattering all around, the other kids leapt to the edges of the room to escape this horrid scene. She found her daughter in the corner, frightened and crying. For a moment, it was bedlam, she said. The teacher finally gained control, and order was restored. Comfort was provided, and I dare say it was addressed again at home. Fathers, and mothers, we cannot always be there to protect them physically. But in this case, as well as many similar times, the emotional scars need addressing to protect and restore her. The boys are another story, as they will need a father to help them get through this in the best possible manner.

And it does not mean we fight our kids' battles for them. And in a similar vein, don't be overprotective. But if a burglar is clearly in your house, it is time for protective and punitive action. We can never shelter our kids from all the wrongs they will encounter. In an earlier chapter, we addressed this somewhat. But when we can see certain perils approaching, we are the ones who should be there to protect and defend. Can you imagine the indescribable comfort your children will feel when they know you are there for them? Here's a possible response: "Man, Dad always has my back. He would be the first one with whom I'd want to go into a dark alley."

It also does not mean you defend them blindly when it is observed that they have brought something on themselves or the family due to their actions or lack thereof. This is a time you as a protector must step in and deal with an injustice in another way. They need to know you still love them, but their actions are to be dealt with and corrective measures need to be implemented. In these cases, you cannot blindly defend your child's actions for the sake of the family or whatever thin reason you might dream up. You will be protecting them from future harm by dealing with it appropriately.

Teaching them to defend themselves, physically and emotionally, is a part of the role also. Today we live in a rather dangerous society in America, worse than any recent time that I can remember. Evil is never predictable. It crops up when least expected, as can be seen in the nightly news. Terrorism on our soil has been introduced into our country as late as ten years ago. How children deal with this psychologically is in your area of responsibility. Helping them cope can be strengthened through open dialogue without adding additional fear. Teach them to be observant, cautious, and aware of their surroundings. Prepare them for certain obvious events that might occur, with you present or not. They, in turn, might be the one who then assists others in a time of need. Teach them to think on their feet and not panic. Have them fully aware and conversant on emergency phone numbers and hotlines.

And I have found the safest place for your kids after a shocking event is snuggled in your arms. Let them talk about it. Do not stifle them just because it might cause tears. Sharing and discussing it will forestall nightmares and lingering emotional suffering and fears. All of this tells us that as the chief protector, you play many roles. Abiding fathers have the best chance of succeeding.

Questions to Ponder

Do you take the role of provider and protector seriously?

What steps do you need to take to ensure the safety and security of your family?

Are you the go-to person in your household for these two areas of responsibility?

How do you need to involve God more in these two areas?

CHAPTER 13:
EVERLASTING FATHER

We are nearing the end of a book about responsible, and hopefully, successful fathering. But as I warned you at the beginning, most of the observations and opinions are from a flawed father, me. And since I have written this series of chapters to those I know to be very similar to me, we should finally spend a few more minutes looking at the most perfect Father. In Isaiah 9:6 NKJV, we see the prophet proclaim the certain coming of the Messiah, the Christ and we know Him as Jesus, as revealed in the Gospels.

"For unto us a Child is born, unto us a Son is given; and the government will be upon His shoulder. And His name will be called Wonderful, Counselor, Mighty God, Everlasting Father, Prince of Peace."

All the roles He has given you as an earthly father are all rolled into these names He holds, but in a more perfect way. Everlasting Father is one that most people do not relate to Jesus, since we see Him as the Son to the Father as we try to visualize the Trinity (Father, Son, and Holy Spirit). But since He is truly God, He is, in fact, our Everlasting Father. Let us be assured that the Spirit made no mistake when He directed Isaiah to speak and record these names of Jesus.

For the next few moments, I will attempt to crystallize the Lord's attributes that are His and that He has deposited into your account to be a father in His image. I will list each chapter and include a scriptural reference to it. It will not even be close to exhaustive, with the hope that it makes you hunger enough to do your own extensive research: (All following scriptures taken from the NKJV.)

Absent: "Lo, I am with you always, even to the end of the age" (Matt. 28:20). "I will never leave you nor forsake you" (Heb. 13:5; Josh. 1:5).

Abiding: "If you abide in Me, and My words abide in you, you will ask what you desire, and it shall be done for you" (John 15:7). "He who dwells in the secret place of the Most High shall abide under the shadow of the Almighty" (Ps. 91:1).

A'loving: "As the father loved Me, I also have loved you; abide in my love" (John 15:9). "Yes, I have loved you with an everlasting love; therefore with lovingkindness I have drawn you" (Jer. 31:3). "For God so loved … that He gave His only begotten Son" (John 3:16).

A'praying: "And when He had sent them away, He departed to the mountain to pray" (Mark 6:46). "And I will pray the Father, and He will give you another Helper, that He may abide with you forever" (John 14:16). "Therefore He is also able to save to the uttermost those who come to God through Him, since He ever lives to make intercession for them" (Heb. 7:25).

A'modeling: "If I then, your Lord and Teacher, have washed your feet, you also ought to wash one another's feet" (John 13:14). "I am the good shepherd. The good shepherd gives his life for his sheep" (John 10:11).

A'mentoring: "Follow Me and I will make you fishers of men" (Matt. 4:19). "Therefore be imitators (followers) of God as dear children" (Eph. 5:1). "And let us run with endurance the race that is set before us, looking unto Jesus, the author and finisher of our faith" (Heb. 12:1b–2a).

A'listening: "Ask, and it shall be given you; seek, and you shall find; knock, and it shall be opened unto you" (Luke 11:9). "If My people who are called by My name will humble themselves, and pray and seek My face, and turn from their wicked ways, then I will hear from heaven, and will forgive their sin and heal their land" (2 Chron. 7:14).

A'teaching: "But the Helper, the Holy Spirit, whom the Father will send in My name, He will teach you all things, and bring to your remembrance all things I have said to you" (John 14:26). "And they were astonished at His teaching, for He taught them as one having authority" (Mark 1:22).

A'disciplining: "My son, do not despise the chastening of the Lord, nor be discouraged when you are rebuked by Him; for whom the Lord loves He chastens, and scourges every son He receives" (Heb. 12:5–6). "For they (earthly fathers) indeed for a few days chastened us as seemed best to them, but He for our profit, that we may be partakers of His holiness" (Heb. 12:10).

A'blessing: 'And as they were eating, Jesus took bread, blessed it and broke it, and gave it to the disciples and said, "Take, eat; this is My body." Then He took the cup … "drink from it, all of you. For this is My blood of the New Covenant, which is shed for many for the remission of sins"' (Matt. 26:26, 28).

A'providing and a'protecting: "And my God shall supply all your needs in Christ Jesus" (Phil. 4:19). "And God is able to make all grace abound toward you, that you, always having all sufficiency in all things, have an abundance for every good work" (2 Cor. 9:8). "As for God, His way is perfect: the word of the Lord is proven; He is a shield for all who trust in Him" (2 Sam. 22:31). "God is my strength and power, and He makes my way perfect" (2 Sam. 22:33). "God is our refuge and strength, a very present help in trouble. Therefore we will not fear" (Ps. 46:1–2a).

The role of father is a difficult but rewarding one. It is obvious God has not given us a responsibility without equipping and empowering us. I find it comforting that everything He has designed for us to be as fathers, He is all of that and far more. In order to ensure success, we need to lean on the *Everlasting Father* for our strength and wisdom to complete the race and to look forward to hearing these words from Him: "Well done!" And maybe also hear your children praising God for their father, *you*. Men—fathers—it is possible!

Questions to Ponder

How can you better emulate the Lord as an abiding father?

How do you stack up in all these areas of fatherhood?

What are your strengths that need to be continued?

What are your weaknesses that need improving?

What is the one most significant lesson you have learned from:
(1) This chapter?

(2) This book?

APPENDIX

Where to start

When you were born, you cried and the world rejoiced. Live your life so that when you die, the world cries and you rejoice.

—Cherokee Expression

Hopefully, you enjoyed reading *From Faith to Faith* and were challenged and blessed by all or some of the material. But we should never lose sight of the overwhelming evidence that the Source and Author of all life, including the family, is God, the Creator. His only Son, Jesus the Christ, was there in the beginning with the Father and the Holy Spirit. Old and New Testament Scriptures speak clearly about the issue. In John 1:3 NASB, the apostle tells us, "All things came into being through Him (Son); and apart from Him nothing came into being that has come into being." He goes on to say in verse 4 that "In Him was life; and the life was the light of men."

And Hebrews 1:1,2 NASB tells us, "God ... in these last days has spoken to us in His Son, whom He appointed heir of all things, through whom also He made the world." Jesus said of Himself in John 14:6 NASB. "I am the way, and the truth, and the life; no one comes to the Father but through Me."

All of His creation speaks of His eternal qualities and majesty. We have but to gaze at the miracles of life each day to see it. Maybe for the first time, or in a deeper sense, you drew nearer to God through the moments you read and pondered on His word. Possibly, He spoke specifically to you, and there is now a desire to know Him more intimately. He said through His servant James in 4:8a that if you "draw near to God and He will draw near to you." How do you do that?

The gospel according to 1 Corinthians 15 is: "Christ died for our sins and rose from the dead." And the Roman road that leads to salvation is: (All scriptures are in the NKJV.)

Romans 3:23 : "For all have sinned and fall short of the glory of God."

Romans 6:23: "For the wages of sin is death, but the free gift of God is eternal life in Jesus Christ our Lord."

Romans 5:8: "But God demonstrates His own love toward us, in that while we were yet sinners, Christ died for us."

Ephesians 2:8–9: "For by grace you have been saved through faith; and that not of yourselves, it is the gift of God; not as a result of works, so that no one may boast."

And in John 5:24 NASB we see a truth that can be embraced through faith (trust) in Jesus who tells you and me, "Truly, truly, I say to you, he who hears My word, and believes Him who sent Me, *has* eternal life, and does not come into judgment, but *has passed* out of death into *life.*" He spoke clearly again in John 11:25 NASB when He said, "I am the resurrection and the life; he who believes in Me shall live even if he dies."

If it is the desire of your heart to trust Jesus Christ for your salvation and to partake in His eternal life, then the following prayer is a suggested way for you to take the step today. Read over the prayer, and if it reflects your wishes, then pray it right now. Know that it is not the prayer that saves, but placing your trust in Christ alone for your salvation.

> Dear God, I know I'm a sinner. I know my sin deserves to be punished. I believe Christ died for me and rose from the grave. I trust Jesus Christ alone as my Savior. Thank You for the forgiveness and everlasting life I now have. In Jesus' name, amen.

Welcome to the Kingdom of God! Did you hear the angels rejoicing? Well, they are!

Eternal life is based on fact, not feeling. Now …

Tell God what is on your mind through prayer (Phil. 4:6–7).

Read the Bible daily (2 Tim. 3:16–17). Start in the book of Philippians or John.

Worship with God's people in a local church (Heb. 10:24–25).

Tell others about Jesus Christ (Matt. 4:19).

Fathers, the best place to start sharing is with your children and spouse. You might even find they have been praying for you for some time. Rejoice together and go enjoy the abundant life of *abiding*, both in the Lord and in the home. Praise God, I no longer have to be absent from the home!

This is my prayer for every reader who has engaged in moving from absent to abiding.

> Father God, I rejoice that You have created us as men and given us the distinct privilege and responsibility to be an abiding father. You are glorified when we as men serve you in the manner You have set forth for us. Thank You for each man who has consciously committed to becoming the best possible father to his children and to love his wife as Christ loves His people. I confess we fail in so many ways, but You know our weaknesses and are there always to encourage and keep us on the right path. Forgive the failures, and strengthen these dedicated fathers. Lord, this is dear to Your heart. Look down on these men, and let them

know You will never leave them nor forsake them. Give them great and glorious success in their role as fathers. May Your Holy Spirit abide in them, and may their families and others see the difference in their lives. I praise You and offer this prayer in the name of Your Son, Jesus. Amen!

I invite you to read the following six testimonies from my friends—fathers, husbands, grandfathers, and great-grandfathers. Reflect on their words of wisdom. All are men I respect and love. Then I challenge you to take a few quiet moments and write your own testimony as a father. You might just surprise yourself. Share it with your children. Then pass this book on to another needy father.

TESTIMONIALS

Elise and I have three sons, two daughters, ten grandsons, four granddaughters, and three great granddaughters.

First, being a father is easier if it is generational. I had a great role model in my father and my grandfather before him. It is a tougher task for someone who does not have that background. I'm not saying it is easy. It was the hardest task I ever had and easily the most rewarding.

Second to that is the role of the mother, for without her influence in parenting decisions, it would be a much heavier load. Father and mother must be as one in their parenting.

Third, it is always a learning experience. While mistakes will be made, you must learn from them or suffer the consequences.

Fourth is to recognize early on that your children need to respect you before they really love you.

Fifth, beginning with the father and mother, strive to teach duty, work, ethics, honor, integrity, respect for the elderly, and love of God and country.

Sixth, it is a fact that your responsibility does not end with childhood, as your children leave home and begin their own lives. They expect you to be there for them, if and when the need arises. Still, you must remember that they have their own lives to live and try not to interfere. No matter what mistakes they might make, they are your children, our greatest legacy, and continue to have our prayers, love, and support.

The greatest reward of parenting is the absolute knowledge that your children love and respect you!

Ronald Sellers
Retired, State Farm Insurance Agency

Cookie and I have four children: our son, Tracy, and three daughters, Kathy Marshall, Allison Cobb, and Linny Gardner. By early in 2010 the family will consist of:

Cookie and I
Four children and their four spouses,
Sixteen grandchildren and eight spouses
Nine great-grandchildren (ages four to zero)

First of all, Cookie and I *wanted* every one of our children. None was a surprise or unexpected. The Lord blessed my occupational efforts, and Cookie never had to or wanted to work outside the home. We wanted to be involved with our family.

As an expression of that, and involved with honoring the Sabbath, when our children were in grade school and junior high school ages, we all agreed that we could do "things" on Sunday provided we all did it together. If we *all* wanted to go to a movie, okay, but one could not go off with friends and leave the rest of us at home, etc.

While flying back from a men's conference in Montreat, North Carolina, it was so loud in the small plane that we were all involved with books and other things. I found my life verse: 3 John 4. "My greatest joy is to know that all my children love the Lord" (or "walk in the way" in some translations). It wasn't easy; Tracy did not come to a profession of faith in Jesus Christ until after foundering through college for two years. The three girls fell into good Bible studies in high school and welcomed Jesus. All four were involved with Campus Crusade in some way during their college years. And today, each of our four couples is active, vocal, energetic, and Christian. Two even put their husbands through seminary (an ordained pastor and an air force chaplain).

One more item, looking back: we never sat down and told our children what kind of a spouse to marry. We prayed a lot, but there were no "standards," no "goals," none of this "just right kind of person" talk. But the Lord handled that so well. Each of our children has just the person to complete him or her. And our joy is that we did not have a hand in it. Did I say all eight are now perfect? Heavens, *no!* We enjoy each couple for just who and what they are. Would we like to see a "little correction" here or there; of course! But that is not part of our duties or responsibilities, and we never mention it—except to ourselves, just the two of us.

Arthur Wood
Retired, New York Life Insurance Company Agency

I have the privilege of being married to a godly praying lady by the name of Eletha. We have a son Marcus, who is married to Shelby, and they are the parents of Marcus II, age six, and Leigh, age one. We are the proud parents of a daughter, age seventeen, who we adopted at birth.

As a father, I realized that the greatest impact I could have on my son was for him to see me loving my wife as Christ loved the church and not to make him (my son) bitter about life. I also understood how important it was to model for my daughter what she should look for in a relationship with a young man.

The most joyful thing my son ever said to me was, "Teach me to be a godly man like you." Marcus is now the youth minister at West Dallas Community Church and a teacher at West Dallas Community School.

What my father passed on to me, I passed on to my son and daughter, which is the importance of loving God and obeying His word. The legacy continues with my grandson, who recently stated, "I read my Bible and pray every day. If I don't, I won't have any strength."

Third John 4 reads "Nothing gives me greater joy than to hear that my children are following the way of truth" (NCV). An absentee father cannot experience this joy.

Arrvel Wilson
Senior Pastor, West Dallas Community Church

My father was never home. He was always drunk, always busy, always making excuses. If it had not been for godly men in my life as a young boy, providing an example of what a man of God was like as a father, I wonder if I would have grown up with the biblical perspective of fatherhood. Our loving heavenly Father, by His incredible grace, has poured into me a passion and commitment for one all-consuming goal as a father, to live each day with the light and love of our Savior coming through me so that my son and daughter can see that Jesus is real and that our faith and trust in Him is the only foundation that will matter in life.

In the 1950s and 1960s, television programs with families consistently showed men who were committed to their families, who were there for their sons and daughters. Desperate for a sense that there were families with loving, concerned fathers, I embraced those wonderful programs that always provided moral lessons and examples for me. Jim Anderson of *Father Knows Best*, played by Robert Young, did not always "know best" and could lose his temper. Yet he was an example to me of loving commitment and dedication to his children. Hugh Beaumont, who played Ward Cleaver in the classic *Leave It to Beaver* provided another example of a rock-solid father who seemed to always be there for his sons. I remember thinking as a child how wonderful it must be to have a father who is home each evening, having a meal with his family, going to his son's school when his son needed him, just being there to listen and give fatherly advice and guidance. Ward Cleaver is often pictured carefully mixing discipline and structure with compassion and understanding as his sons struggled with mistakes and poor judgment common with our own children.

Our Heavenly Father is like that, gently and lovingly reminding us, as fathers, of the importance of being there, as He is always there for us. God reminds us that His Word is a guide and roadmap for our journey as fathers, providing the structure and warnings of danger with the reminder of His unconditional love for us. As fathers, we may be disappointed and even angry with decisions our children make, but by God's grace, we must never forget the power of unconditional love toward them. There is no circumstance too painful, no relationship too strained or damaged that it can't be mended with the continual expression of our love, unconditionally, to the sons and daughters God has given to us.

One of the great examples of a godly father was the father chosen by Jesus to illustrate the Heavenly Father in the parable we reference as the parable of the "Prodigal Son." This was father was *approachable*, as his young son felt the freedom to come to his father and tell him of his desire to find his new life in a "far away country." He was *approachable* even from the pig pen, as his son declared, "I will arise and go to my father." He was a father who in his son's mind was *associated with heaven,* as his son declared "I have sinned against heaven and before you." His son would not be reminded of God without thinking of his father, who surely walked with God, who prayed, whose life was an open book revealing the fruit of the spirit: love, kindness, gentleness, humility, and forgiveness. And the parable clearly shows he was a father who was *affectionate,* as Jesus tells us the father "ran and fell on his neck and kissed him." It is a lie, utter nonsense, to say that "manhood" calls for coldness and no emotions. Godly fathers freely express their love and aren't afraid to make the first move … or even risk rejection. The prodigal son's father did not say, "I told you so," because *as a godly father, he valued the relationship more than "being right" and the son knew it!* One son's failures did not remove him from his father's love, just as our failures do not remove us from our Father's love.

Len McLaughlin
Former President, SNB Bank
Now Senior Pastor and Founder, Heritage Church

In reflecting on our five adult children and their training, these are five observations I'll make as a father:

1) "Unless the Lord builds the house its builders labor in vain" (Ps. 127:1). Keeping God first is an on-going process, especially in a Dad's life.

2) Loving their mother next to the Lord never gets less important both as a purpose and example.

3) I agreed with my wife that our overall training goal was that each child would seek God's will and do it in his or her individual life (remember not to expect

behavior out of the season for the time of life he or she is in, such as requiring adult behavior from an adolescent).

4) All the "one anothers" in Ephesians are very important to seek and apply first in God's primary small group, the family (love, forgive, patience, etc.).

5) Pray with reference to observation number one. Now with five married children and thirteen grandchildren, each year someone in the family compiles a list of each member's prayer requests for our family to lift up.

Ford Madison
Real Estate Investor

I grew up in Raleigh, Ashville, Washington DC, and Atlanta. My dad worked for IBM, which we learned early on stands for, "I've Been Moved!" I had a great dad who taught me, by lifelong personal example, the values of faithfully and passionately loving my mom (his bride of sixty years!), loving his family, leading us to weekly worship, diligence and excellence at work, and the importance of fun, rest, and recreation. He took us on countless family outings and vacations that created deep and lasting family bonds of unity and love. Ultimately, he demonstrated for me the three greatest gifts that a father can give to his children. Now I am seeking to pass those three gifts on to my own children.

The Three Greatest Gifts

The First Gift. I believe that the greatest gift I can ever give my children as their father is to love God with all my heart, mind, soul, and strength by walking with Him daily and obeying His word and His will for my life. Jesus says, "If a man abides in Me and I in him, he will bear much fruit; apart from Me you can do nothing" (John 15:5). The fruit of the heritage of healthy, well-adjusted, and godly children can only result from a father walking with God. When I love Him right, I will live rightly, and as a result, all human relationships (especially those within the home) will take their right order under His direction, wisdom, order, and plan. As I am filled daily and submit to His Holy Spirit, I will demonstrate the fruit of His Spirit living within me: "love, joy, peace, patience, kindness, goodness, faithfulness, gentleness and self-control" (Gal. 5:22–23). What greater heritage could any father give his children than to set a lifelong example of what it really looks like to walk uprightly with God? There is no greater gift that a father can give his children than this!

The Second Gift. I believe that the second greatest gift that a father can give his children is to love their mother faithfully for life! Pat and I go on weekly dates and quarterly weekend "escapes" where we cultivate our love for one another and enjoy being together alone (spelled "r-o-m-a-n-c-e"). During these date nights and getaways, we pray together for our children and prayerfully discuss and plan for their welfare. Pat is my number one love (after Jesus, of course), and that gives my children not only great security as they witness our faithful love for one another as husband and wife, but it also gives them a great example of fidelity and purity to strive to follow in their own marriages. We have the responsibility and the privilege of painting a picture over the canvas of a lifetime that reflects the beauty of biblical love and the marriage covenant as God, the architect, designed them to be!

The Third Gift. I believe that the third greatest gift that a father can give his children is his presence and his time. This one is tough for the twenty-first-century, high-tech, high-demand, high-stress, and very busy American dad! But it is equally as critical as the first two gifts. Every child needs Dad (and Mom) to be emotionally and chronologically present in their lives. This is an "ever striving, never fully realized" type of challenge. But never cease striving to get this one right!

For our family, this starts with dinner together around the dinner table as often as we can with Dad present. It also includes Dad making pancakes or waffles on weekend mornings whenever possible. Family vacations, family fun nights, and outings to parks, museums, concerts, plays, fairs, and the like are all very important for family times with Dad. However, there is also the need in every child for one-on-one connection with their father. With nine children, this one was the hardest challenge for us, as you could imagine! Whether it is "date night" with Dad and daughter or dinner and activity with father and son, singling each child out for focused one-on-one time with their father is absolutely essential. Even while at home, fathers need to find ways of connecting personally with each child one on one. Often listening to the events of the child's day, praying together with a child for his or her hurts and hopes and dreams, and giving advice (when sought or asked for) are great ways to build that special one-on-one between a father and each child.

Bruce Johnston taught me to ask my younger children at bedtime to share with me the "bright spot" and the "dark spot" of the day. This routine has been a fantastic window into their world and a great way to close each day in prayer as they reflect upon their highs and lows that day. I also highly recommend taking each child while in their teenage years to a father-child camping experience like the JH Ranch in Etna, California, which has a brilliantly designed program to "turn the hearts of the fathers to their children and the children to their fathers" (Mal. 4:6).

May God grant you favor and success in your calling to show the heart, hands, and face of your heavenly Father to your children as their earthly daddy! Godspeed!

Kurt Nelson
President, East-West Ministries International

Questions to Ponder:

What would be your short summation on the attributes of fathering?

Have you ever written out a testimony of your life?

What insight into your role as a father do you think you would gain by writing these?

After you have completed these, would you share them with your family?

NOTES

1   Theodore Roosevelt, "Citizenship in a Republic" (speech, Sorbonne, Paris, April 23, 1910).

2   "Unwed Birth Rate Reaches All-time High in U.S., last modified March 18, 2009, http://www.msnbc.msn.com/id/29754561/ns/health-womens_health/

3   Roosevelt, "Citizenship in a Republic."

4   "Births Outside Marriage: The Real Story," last modified November 24, 2009, http://www.esrc.ac.uk/ESRCInfoCentre/about/CI/CP/the_edge/issue8/births_1.aspx

5   Ibid.

6   Ibid.

7   William Julius Wilson, When Work Disappears (New York: Alfred A. Knopf, 1996).

8   Lorrie Irby Jackson, "How Single Moms Can Hurt Their Kids," last modified August 14, 2009,http://www.dallasnews.com/sharedcontent/dws/dn/opinion/viewpoints/stories/DN-jackson_15edi.State.Edition1.45ff22.html

9   "Our Opinion: Statistics Paint Bleak Picture of Fatherless, Children," last modified June 20, 2009, http://www.timesrecordnews.com/news/2009/jun/20/life-without-dad-statistics-paint-bleak-picture/

10   M.L. Menchen, The American Language, 1945.

11   WordNet Dictionary, s.v. "absent." http://www.webster-dictionary.org/definition/absent

12 Harry Chapin, "Cat's in the Cradle", 1974. Used by Permission. [Bill use the required documentation specified at the end of the permission letter you received.]

13 Attributed to Chinese philosopher Lao-tzu (c. 604-c 531 bc), founder of Taoism.

14 WordNet Dictionary, s.v. "abide." http://www.webster-dictionary. org/definition/abide

15 Attributed to Daniel Webster in an address delivered to the New York Historical Society on February 23, 1852.

16 Attributed to Ron Wild.

17 John Hendricks Bechtel, Slips of Speech: A Helpful Book for Everyone Who Aspires to Correct the Everyday Errors of Speaking (Salt Lake City: Project Gutenberg, 2004), 29.

18 Access www.YouTube.com and type in: Ironman and Dick and Rick Hoyt.

19 The saying has been credited to American military officer and politician Lewis Cass (1782-1866), but there is no evidence that he said it.

20 WordNet Dictionary, s.v. "model." http://www.webster-dictionary. org/definition/model

21 WordNet Dictionary, s.v. "mentor." http://www.webster- dictionary. org/definition/mentor

22 Attributed to Robert McCloskey, U.S. State Department spokesman, by Marvin Kalb, CBS reporter, in *TV Guide*, 31 March 1984, citing an unspecified press briefing during the Vietnam war.

23 WordNet Dictionary, s.v. "blessing." http://www.webster-dictionary. org/definition/blessing

AUTHOR BIO

BILL C. DOTSON founded Dallas Real Estate Ministries (DREM) in 1986 when God placed a calling on his life, along with eleven other men. The mandate was to "build a spiritual house" in the real estate community of Dallas, Texas, in accordance with 1 Peter 2:4–5. The marketplace ministry is dedicated to drawing men and women to Jesus Christ. After fifty years in the real estate industry, Bill is currently the executive director of DREM (www.drem.org). Natives of Franklin, Tennessee, Bill and his wife, Joanne, now live in Dallas. They have two married daughters and five grandchildren. Each month Bill also writes and publishes *Life Speaks to Us* (www.lifespeakstous.com) and has published a book of the same title through CrossBooks Publishing.